CPL.

Field Airgun Shooting

JAMES MARCHINGTON

Pelham Books
London

To my wife, Sara.

PELHAM BOOKS

Published by the Penguin Group
27 Wrights Lane, London W8 5TZ, England
Viking Penguin Inc., 40 West 23rd Street, New York 10010, USA
Penguin Books Australia Ltd, Ringwood, Victoria, Australia
Penguin Books Canada Ltd, 2801 John Street, Markham, Ontario, Canada L3R 1B4
Penguin Books (NZ) Ltd, 182–190 Wairau Road, Auckland 10, New Zealand

Penguin Books Ltd, Registered Offices: Harmondsworth, Middlesex, England

First published 1988

Copyright © James Marchington 1988

Typeset by Cambrian Typesetters, Frimley, Surrey
Printed and bound by Butler and Tanner Ltd, Frome

British Library Cataloguing in Publication Data

Marchington, James
  Field airgun shooting.
  1. Field air gun shooting
  I. Title
  799.2'028'3

ISBN 0–7207–1823–6

Contents

Foreword

by Paul Dobson, Editor of *Air Gunner Magazine*

Airguns have advanced in leaps and bounds during the past decade, and just as the weapons have become increasingly sophisticated so too has the sport of airgun shooting.

Not so many years ago airgunning was widely regarded as little more than a stepping stone along the path to the more adult shooting sports, providing youngsters with their first chance of owning a gun and learning the shooting safety code.

How things have changed! Today airgunning has blossomed into a full-blown sport in its own right, giving shooters the opportunity to use their air rifles for hunting small quarry, taking part in field target competitions or improving their skills shooting targets and tin cans in the garden.

Much of the credit for this progress is due to the world's gunmakers and scope manufacturers, who have raised the standard of the equipment within a remarkably short space of time. Without their talent and ingenuity the sport could not have developed so rapidly or become so popular as it has done.

A keen shot all his life, James Marchington has monitored the sport's growth at first hand, testing most of the new rifles, pistols and scopes to arrive on the market and checking their potential in true field conditions.

James is a genuine countryman, too, and his unique appreciation of wildlife and the changing seasons, and his long experience of the attributes required by an airgun hunter, will prove invaluable to those who enjoy the prospect of field shooting.

This excellent book, covering the many aspects of airgun shooting, is long overdue and will be warmly welcomed by all those who read it. My only regret is that it was not available when I was embarking on a shooting career!

Section I

FIELD AIRGUNS AND EQUIPMENT

1. Development of the modern airgun

The modern airgun is a highly sophisticated machine, capable of sending a pellet speeding towards its target with amazing accuracy. It will kill a rabbit cleanly, or knock over a solid metal target, at ranges of 40 yards or more, provided the shooter can hold it steady enough. In fact, it is probably fair to say that today's airgunner is limited not by his gun, but by his ability to shoot it accurately.

Airguns are often thought of as toys, or the first step in a novice's progression to a 'real' gun – a cartridge rifle or shotgun. This is largely because the airguns in general use a generation or two ago were relatively weak and inaccurate, and considered suitable only for the fairground shooting stall or for plinking at tin cans in the garden. This was not always the case, however. Earlier in its development, the airgun has been used as a serious hunting weapon, and a type of airgun was even used with great success by the Austrian Army at the end of the eighteenth century.

Looking further back in time, the blowpipe is the earliest weapon which is recognisable as a type of airgun. The pipe itself is the barrel, and the shooter's lungs provide the air which sends the projectile on its way. Blowpipes are still in use today, and most people will have come across the schoolboy's version, the pea-shooter. With practice it is possible to fire a bullet or dart from a blowpipe quite accurately, and the power can be sufficient to kill or stun a small animal at a reasonable range – although man soon discovered that a dose of poison on the tip of the dart improved his chances of filling the bag.

Other methods of firing a projectile tended to steal the limelight, however, with longbows, crossbows and, later, gunpowder proving to be a more effective way of killing an enemy or putting game in the pot. But throughout history we see air-powered weapons appearing in one form or another.

AIR RESERVOIR GUNS

The earliest weapons which can be described as true airguns are those with an air reservoir, often in the stock. Some of the earliest examples known today came from Nuremberg in the early 1500s, and even in those early days airguns were disapproved of by the authorities because of their quiet but deadly operation.

Many of these early airguns were made to look like the firearms of the time, and in the early eighteenth century we see 'flintlock' airguns which had a hammer, pan and frizzen. You could even put gunpowder in the pan, which would ignite when the gun was fired, although it did not help to propel the bullet.

At around the same time the bellows type of airgun was being developed. In some ways, this was the beginning of the spring airgun that is so familiar today. The other airguns of the time relied on a reservoir of air which was charged up with a pump some time before the shot was fired. On the other hand with the bellows airgun the air was compressed by spring power when you pulled the trigger. You cocked the bellows mechanism in the stock with the aid of a special key. Pulling the trigger released the spring, which squeezed the leather bellows and compressed the air inside to fire the pellet.

It was also around this time that the ball shaped reservoir first appeared. The ball was removed and charged with a separate pump, then screwed back onto the gun to fire a number of shots before it had to be recharged. By carrying a spare ball, you could fire many shots before charging again.

The Austrian Army used repeating air rifles of .44 calibre from 1780 to 1815. These guns had a detachable stock air reservoir which contained sufficient compressed air for about twenty shots, and the soldiers carried spare stocks to give them greater firepower. The bullets were held in a tubular magazine, and these airguns could be reloaded much faster than the more conventional firearms used by their enemies.

AIR CANES

The notorious air cane appeared on the scene around the middle of the nineteenth century. This type of airgun was made to look like an ordinary walking stick, but could fire a large calibre ball with devastating power. Being easily concealed, and virtually silent in use, air canes earned a reputation as the weapon of poachers and murderers.

Another interesting airgun which appeared around this time was the 'crank wound' type – the first to use the configuration of spring, piston and cylinder that you find in spring airguns today. The crank was used to cock the mainspring, and consisted of a handle with a cogwheel which engaged a toothed rack connected to the piston. By turning the handle, you would draw the piston back against the pressure of the mainspring, until eventually it reached the full cock position and engaged the trigger. You had to remove the crank handle before firing, of course, otherwise it would fly round as the piston moved forwards in the cylinder.

Many of today's high-powered air rifles follow the same basic design as the early spring airguns. The break-barrel system, in which the barrel is used as a lever to compress the spring, has been with us for years, and will no doubt still be popular for a long time to come. It has proved itself to be reliable and effective, and has the advantage that it is completely self-contained. There is no need to carry a separate charger or air supply, because the power is replenished each time you cock the gun. Modern engineering methods have overcome some of the early problems with break-barrel guns, such as ensuring that the barrel comes up aligned precisely with the cylinder every time, and today's high-tech plastics have solved the problem of sealing the breech effectively.

Gunsmiths and airgunners are an ingenious lot, however, and never satisfied with the performance of their weapons. Many alternative systems have been tried, with varying degrees of success. Some ideas never made it off the drawing board, others fell by the wayside before they were ever taken up by a manufacturer for mass production, and still more have enjoyed a brief rise to fame only to fade away again.

One of the fascinating things about the history of gunmaking – and many other subjects as well, for that matter – is the way that similar designs crop up many years apart and in totally different areas of the world. Sometimes this is because new materials and methods allow an earlier design to be made more effective, while in other cases two minds have come up with a similar answer to the same problems.

An example is the air cartridge design. Paul Giffard, an engineer living in Paris in the nineteenth century, patented an air cartridge system for air canes, rifles and pistols. The idea was not followed up, and seemed set to disappear into the pages of history. In recent years, however, Saxby and Palmer have developed their own air cartridge system, using a pre-charged air cartridge in various air rifles and pistols. The cartridges are charged with a hand pump, and you can carry a good number of them in a pocket or in a looped belt similar to a shotgun cartridge belt. This avoids the need to re-charge or cock your gun after each shot, as it is a simple matter to operate the bolt to eject the spent cartridge and load a fresh one. You have to be careful to retrieve the empty cartridge, of course, because they are not cheap to replace.

RECENT DEVELOPMENTS

In Chapter 3 we will examine the various types of airgun and their particular merits, but for the moment let us look at some other examples of the more interesting recent developments.

Theoben Engineering produce a break-barrel rifle which works in exactly the same way as a spring airgun with one vital difference – it has no spring. Instead, there is an inert gas sealed in the space behind the piston, and this is compressed by cocking just as a spring would be. More about this interesting weapon in Chapter 3.

Great strides have been taken in the area of pneumatic airguns recently, particularly the pre-charged type. This has several advantages over airguns that you have to pump up after every few shots. Most important to my mind is the fact that pumping an airgun involves a certain amount of physical effort, and usually leaves you in no fit state to shoot accurately.

The Saxby and Palmer pre-charged air cartridge system, described above, is one answer, but even the straightforward pre-charged pneumatic airgun has been the subject of much improvement lately, with one of the most promising ideas being the addition of a second air reservoir which provides a kind of stepping stone between the main reservoir and the barrel. This means that the gun shoots more consistently, because the pressure in the second reservoir can be controlled accurately to the same level for each shot, even when the pressure in the main reservoir starts to drop.

THE FUTURE

So where will airguns go from here? I will stick my neck out and say that I believe pre-charged pneumatics are the guns of the future. I think that more sophisticated valve systems and improved triggers will make these guns even more accurate and consistent than they are now. Despite the fact that they require a separate pump for charging, I believe that pre-charged pneumatics will be seen more and more both in competitions and in the field.

That is not to say that spring-powered airguns will disappear – far from it. The spring airgun has been around a long time, and has been developed to such an extent that it offers all the power and accuracy that most shooters can use. It is also a relatively simple design to manufacture, which helps to make these guns available at a price the average shooter can afford.

While I am indulging in this crystal ball gazing, let me also say that I expect to see a few other changes to airgunning as we know it today. Pressure from the anti-field sports brigade will increase, and I shan't be at all surprised if we find ourselves fighting for our rights to shoot live quarry with airguns – and even to own and carry an airgun without some form of certificate. Lead pellets are likely to come in for some criticism on environmental grounds, and we can expect to be looking round for alternative ammunition before too long.

One thing is certain. So long as airguns are around, there will be people who want to see them banned – and it is up to us, today's airgunners, to see that we behave responsibly enough to ensure that the next generation can still enjoy this great sport.

2. How an airgun works

If you're going to be a good driver, you need to have a basic understanding of how a car works, and the same principle applies to airgun shooting. It is possible to shoot reasonably well without knowing a sear from a piston, but the more you know about your weapon the better you will be able to deal with any problems you may have – and the more satisfaction you will gain from your shooting.

As I said in the previous chapter, an airgun consists of two main parts: the barrel down which the pellet travels for the first part of its journey, and the power source which provides compressed air to propel the pellet. That description applies equally to the simple blowpipe or the most sophisticated modern competition gun.

To be much use, an airgun will also need a stock so that you can hold it steady, and some form of sighting system to help you line up the barrel with the target. Once again, these can be very simple or very complicated, and don't assume that more complicated means better. Very often a simple set of iron sights, for example, can do just as good a job as an expensive optical sight, and they don't have such delicate parts to break down at the wrong moment.

THE BREAK-BARREL SYSTEM

Let's look at a typical airgun and see how the various parts work. For my example, I have taken a straightforward spring powered break-barrel design which most shooters will instantly recognise. In the next chapter we will examine variations on this theme.

We will start with the cylinder and piston, since this is the heart of the airgun. The cylinder is basically a length of round metal tube with a polished inside surface. The piston is a snug fit inside the cylinder, and can slide up and down it. On the end of the piston is some form of airtight seal, so that when the piston moves forward it pushes the air in front of it up the cylinder – otherwise the air would escape around the edges. Until quite recently, a leather washer was used to provide this seal, but nowadays most manufacturers use plastics such as neoprene.

Behind the piston is a powerful spring which is held in place by a plug at the rear end of the cylinder. When the piston is pushed backwards, this compresses the spring and stores up mechanical energy which is released when you pull the trigger.

To compress the spring takes a lot of effort, so you need to have a lever which makes the job easier. This is provided by the barrel, which hinges on a pin at the front of the cylinder. A cocking link connects the barrel to the piston, so that when you pull the barrel downwards it pushes the piston back and compresses the spring.

When the piston reaches the furthest point, it catches on the sear of the trigger mechanism. This holds the piston in the cocked position until you release it by pulling the trigger. Once you have loaded a pellet in the breech and closed the barrel, the gun is ready to fire.

On firing, the energy of the spring is released, and the piston rushes forward, compressing the air in the cylinder rather like a bicycle pump. There is only one way for the air to escape, and that is through the transfer port which leads to the barrel. An air seal prevents any leakage of air around the breech, so the air pushes the pellet up the barrel and out towards the target. The pellet is a tight fit in the breech, so considerable pressure builds up behind it before it begins to move.

Anyone who has paid attention in physics lessons will know that when you compress a gas, you also raise its temperature and this is the cause of one of the most common airgun problems: dieselling. Airguns need to be lubricated so that the piston and spring do not suffer from too much friction, which would reduce the power drastically. Most novices are inclined to get carried away with lubrication, and splash oil far too liberally around the cylinder. When the air is compressed and the temperature rises sharply, this oil can vaporise and ignite, causing a small explosion inside the cylinder. The gun goes off with a loud 'crack', rather like a cartridge rifle, and the pellet is ejected at a much higher velocity than normal.

This might be desirable except for three things. First, it is illegal, because technically a dieselling air rifle requires a firearms certificate. Second, it will quite probably damage the gun, which is not built to withstand the much higher pressures involved. And third, dieselling is highly unpredictable. You can never be sure whether a gun will diesel or not, and even when it does the velocity of the pellet can vary enormously, making it impossible to predict the pellet's trajectory. The moral is, don't over-lubricate your airgun, and never put any oil in front of the piston, only behind it around the spring.

Cardew's combustion theory

This leads me to an interesting theory developed by Gerald Cardew, who believes that spring airguns owe at least some of their power to burning lubricants. Cardew has shown by scientific experiments that a spring airgun develops more power than can be explained purely by the effect of compressing the air in the cylinder. His theory states that a tiny amount of oil finds its way into the cylinder each time the gun is cocked, and this burns when the gun is fired, adding the extra power. If too much oil finds its way into the cylinder, then it explodes instead of burning, and the result is dieselling. Cardew has shown that when all the oil is removed from a gun's cylinder, its power drops drastically – which would seem to support his theory. His experiments with different types of piston seal show that some help to 'wick' forward the correct amount of oil, and produce a more powerful, consistent gun.

Cardew's theory is fascinating, but whether you believe it or not will make no difference to how your gun performs, just so long as you take care to lubricate it properly.

PNEUMATIC AIRGUNS

The Cardew theory is only relevant to spring airguns, of course. Pneumatic airguns work on an entirely different principle. Instead of a spring and piston which compresses the air when you fire, compressed air is stored in a reservoir behind the pellet, and held there by a valve. When you pull the trigger, the valve releases air from the reservoir which propels the pellet down the barrel. This valve is the vital part of a pneumatic airgun. In order to do its job properly, it must be totally airtight until the moment the trigger is pulled. When that happens, it must release the air instantly and smoothly, without restricting its flow and slowing the pellet. Modern plastics have replaced the old materials such as animal horn which were used for sealing valves, and the results are longer life and greater efficiency.

There are two basic types of valve, depending on the type of airgun. The first is the 'dump' type, which is so called because it remains open when you fire, dumping all the air in the reservoir. This is used in airguns which need to be pumped up again for each shot.

The second type opens for a fraction of a second and allows only part of the air out of the reservoir, leaving enough pressure inside for further shots before recharging. This type of gun has the advantage that you can fire several shots before you need to pump it up again, but the power tends to fall off with each shot. More recently, engineers have developed a pneumatic airgun with two reservoirs connected by a valve. The main reservoir is used to 'top up' the smaller one, and the contents of the second reservoir can be 'dumped' with each shot. The idea is to combine the advantages of both types of pneumatic, to provide a gun which will fire many shots before recharging, but will give consistent shot-to-shot power.

THE STOCK

Earlier in this chapter, I dismissed the stock as simply a means of holding the gun steady – and so it is, but there is a lot more to it than that.

In shotgun shooting, the stock is all-important, because it determines whether or not the gun will shoot where you point it. This is because a shotgun has no rearsight. Effectively, the shooter's eye is the rearsight, and its position in relation to the barrels is critical. When you shoot at a moving target with a shotgun, you bring the gun up to the aim as your body swings with the target, and you fire almost immediately the butt touches your shoulder. There is no time to check that you are looking straight down the barrels, so it is vital that the gun fits you well and comes up to the aim correctly every time.

This is not so important for airgun shooting, because your target is stationary and there is time to aim more carefully, lining up the rearsight, foresight and target. Even so, a well-fitted stock can make it easier to shoot accurately, because it will be more comfortable to aim the gun.

Gun stocks are traditionally made from walnut or similar wood, which is both strong and attractive to look at. Here again, modern materials are tending to replace the old, although in this case I am not so sure it is an improvement. A plastic stock may make a gun cheaper to manufacture, but to my mind it does nothing for its looks.

The important dimensions of a stock are the length, the height at the comb, and the cast-off. Length is obvious enough. This is the distance between the trigger and the butt – and it is actually the least important measurement. Provided it is long enough to keep the scope away from your face, and not so long that you have to stretch for the trigger, then you need not worry about your stock's length.

More important is the height at the comb. This is the point where your cheek touches the stock, and it determines whether or not your eye will fall naturally in line with the sights. Virtually every airgun on the market is designed so that it can be used with either open sights or a scope. This means that the stock must be low enough at the comb to allow you to see the open sights clearly – and that puts your eye too low when you fit a scope, because a scope is higher above the barrel than open sights. If you plan to use your gun with a scope all the time, it could well be worthwhile adding an extension to the comb so that your eye is aligned with the centre of the scope when you rest your cheek comfortably on the stock.

The other stock measurement I mentioned was the cast-off. This is more relevant to shotguns, and is the degree of bend in the stock which allows you to keep your head upright while you look down the barrel. Very few airguns have any cast-off. A normal airgun stock will be dead straight, with the result that you have to tilt your head to one side – to the right if you are right-handed – to line up the sights. This is not a great problem, but if you decide to have a custom stock made specially to fit you, it would be worth bearing in mind. Apart from sheer comfort, it would be easier to judge when the rifle is exactly vertical.

THE TRIGGER

We have already looked at the cylinder and the piston and spring inside, but what of the trigger? Triggers vary enormously from the very simple to unbelievably complex. At its simplest, a trigger is a catch which engages a notch on the piston. There is a spring to push it into position when the piston is pulled back, and a trigger blade for you to pull when you want to release it. This very simple form of trigger would be clumsy to operate, however, and it would wear quickly and become unsafe.

The ideal trigger holds the piston very securely, but releases it with a light pressure of the trigger finger. It should be adjustable so you can vary the trigger pressure to suit your style of shooting, but it should be safe even when set on the minimum pressure. When you pull it, you should not feel any slip or 'creep'. Instead, it should remain steady as you build up the pressure gradually, until it suddenly releases.

You will see that with the simplest form of trigger, the only way to vary the trigger pressure needed to release it is to alter the sear engagement. This means that on the lowest pressure, the sear is only just catching the notch on the piston, and a slight knock will jar the sear out and allow the gun to go off. What is needed is a more complicated mechanism which will allow the sear to be fully engaged even when the trigger is set to a very light pressure. Many shooters also like to have some slack on the trigger, so they can pull it back for a short distance before they come up against the actual trigger pressure. This is known as a double-pull trigger, and is a different thing from trigger 'creep'. It is found on some of the more expensive competition guns.

A really good trigger is quite a tall order for the engineers, and many different types of mechanism have been tried with varying degrees of success. One of the most highly regarded is the Weihrauch 'Rekord' trigger which is fitted on the popular Weihrauch hunting rifles such as the HW80 and HW77.

THE BARREL

The barrel is another part which appears simple at first sight, but is actually rather complicated. It might look like a straight-forward metal tube, but the modern airgun barrel is a master-piece of engineering. Many people imagine that the barrel is the same from one end to the other, but this is not the case. The breech has to be slightly oversize to allow you to insert the pellet without damaging it. This end of the barrel also requires an effective seal to prevent air escaping when you fire. This often takes the form of a rubber or plastic O-ring set into the end of the barrel, which is pinched against the cylinder when the gun is closed. It is a good idea to check this seal regularly for signs of damage, and replace it if it looks worn.

Immediately past the breech the rifling starts. This consists of a set of grooves cut into the inside surface, which form a slow spiral along the length of the barrel. The soft lead pellet is pushed into these grooves, which then set it spinning as it travels down the barrel. It continues to spin as it flies towards the target, and this helps to keep it on a straight path – rather like a gyroscope. The number of grooves, their depth and their pitch – the number of turns per metre of barrel – are carefully calculated to give the optimum result.

Some barrels also vary in bore along their length, becoming tighter as the pellet moves towards the muzzle. This has been shown to make the gun more consistent and accurate, and it is used by some manufacturers such as Anschutz of Germany.

Finally, the muzzle, which is simply the business end of the barrel. This part is easily forgotten, but it can make or break the gun's performance. Any imperfection at the muzzle will give the pellet a nudge off-course, and undo all the good work done along the way by the rest of the gun. The muzzle must be properly 'crowned', or finished off, so that it allows the pellet to continue its journey unaffected. This is a skilled job, and it is one reason why an amateur should never attempt to shorten a barrel himself.

AIRGUN SIGHTS

This is a huge subject and so much so that I have devoted a whole chapter to it later in the book. For the moment, suffice to say that most airguns come fitted with simple open sights consisting of a notch rearsight and a blade foresight. These are normally adjustable up and down (elevation) and side to side (windage).

In order to understand how adjusting the sights affects the point of impact of the pellet, you must think of an imaginary line drawn from rearsight to foresight and on towards the target. Because light travels in a straight line, this line of sight is dead straight – unlike the pellet's flight which is curved. The pellet drops faster and faster the further it travels from the muzzle, so the line of flight or trajectory starts as an almost straight line, and becomes increasingly curved until eventually the pellet runs out of steam altogether and drops straight towards the earth.

Using open sights

It stands to reason that the line of sight and the trajectory cannot follow the same path – one is straight while the other is curved. If you choose a given range, though, you can arrange things so that the two lines cross at the same point – in other words, the pellet hits the point that the sights are aiming at. Adjusting the sights to achieve this at a given range is called zeroing. I will discuss this further in Chapter 11.

For the meantime, all you need to understand is that when you adjust the rearsight, the point of impact moves in the same direction. For example, if you move the rearsight down by adjusting the screw, the pellet will hit lower on the target. I always find it easier to understand if I imagine the line of sight to be fixed, and adjusting the sight tilts the rifle in relation to it. In practice, this is what actually happens, because once you have adjusted the sight you line up again on the target. The sights are still aimed at the same point, and the rifle is tilted slightly differently.

These, then, are the basic principles which are the same in any airgun you care to name. Returning to the analogy of a motor car, every make and model from a Mini to a Ferrari works in basically the same way. There are many variations, though, and different guns, like different cars, are designed for specific purposes. Some are relatively cheap and utilitarian, while others are built for ultimate performance with no expense spared. In the following chapter, we look at some of the different types, and see how each is suited to its particular purpose.

3.   Types of airgun

This unusual gun is actually a BSA Scorpion action set in a cut-off Buccaneer stock. The sight is a Singlepoint red dot sight.

In the previous chapter I described the simplest examples of 'typical' airguns of the spring-powered and pneumatic variety. Within these basic categories there are many variations. A spring-powered airgun may be cocked by the barrel, or with a separate under- or side-lever, for example. It may have a tap or sliding breech, and may even be fitted with a pellet feed mechanism to help you load more quickly. And if you look at the advertisements in the various airgun magazines, you will find that the different manufacturers make all kinds of claims about the benefits of their particular models. Even quite a small local gunshop may have dozens of different airguns to choose from.

It makes quite a bewildering selection. How can you tell which gun is best for your particular type of shooting? After all, a mistake is likely to prove expensive. The short answer is that virtually any airgun you care to name is very good in its own field. Provided you choose one which is designed for your

branch of the sport, the choice is up to you and your own personal preferences. By and large you get what you pay for, and the more you can afford to spend, the better finished and more accurate a gun you can buy. One important piece of advice is not to go for power above all else. Power is certainly important if you plan to shoot live quarry, or knock over steel silhouette targets consistently. But most modern airguns have more than enough power for this purpose. All the power in the world is wasted if your shot misses its target, however, so the first priority is to make sure that you can shoot accurately with your chosen gun. Here again, the better examples of modern airguns are capable of tremendous accuracy, and most of them are capable of shooting far more accurately and consistently than the average airgunner!

The different mechanisms have their advantages and dis-advantages, however, and you can make things easier for yourself by choosing the gun which best matches your type of shooting.

BREAK-BARREL GUNS

The break-barrel system is probably the best known, as it has been the standard airgun design for several decades. For this reason it has also been well and truly proven in the field, and today's break-barrel guns are some of the most reliable available.

The break-barrel design suffers from one or two potential disadvantages, however. First, the breech seal must be very effective so that air is not lost around the breech when you fire, which would cause a drop in power. The rubbery plastics used for modern breech seals are excellent, and last a long time without leaking. They can still be damaged by careless use, however, and you should make a habit of checking the breech seal regularly. If it shows any signs of damage, you should replace it. A new one will cost only a few pence, and it will be well worthwhile to keep your gun operating at its best.

Another possible disadvantage of the break-barrel airgun is that the barrel is not fixed in relation to the cylinder, so the locking mechanism has to be very precise to make sure that the barrel always closes in exactly the same position each time. If it does not, then the sights may not be lined up properly with the barrel – causing you to miss the target. Most break-barrel guns have the rearsight fitted to the breech end of the barrel, rather than on the cylinder, so even if the barrel is aligned differently for each shot, the sights are still right. But a scope is usually fitted on the cylinder, so barrel 'droop' would cause trouble.

In practice, modern airgun manufacturers have more or less

overcome this problem with very effective spring-loaded catch mechanisms, so you need not worry about it unless your gun develops a fault.

Cocking a break-barrel airgun can sometimes be difficult, particularly if you are shooting prone – that is, lying on your stomach. In order to pull the barrel back far enough to cock the gun, you will have to roll onto your side, positioning your body again once you have finished. This can be awkward when you are stalking live quarry and want to re-load with the minimum of disturbance.

Some of the older break-barrel guns suffered from weak barrels, and the strain of cocking them over and over again eventually caused the barrel to bend, so the gun shot lower as time went by. Once again modern materials have solved the problem, so that is one less thing you need to worry about when choosing a gun.

One interesting development of the break-barrel design is the Theoben Sirocco, a solidly built, British gun which looks exactly like an ordinary break-barrel weapon, but uses compressed gas instead of a spring. The gas is sealed in the cylinder behind the piston, and it is compressed by the piston when you cock the gun, in exactly the same way as a conventional spring. The gas has certain advantages over a metal spring. It does not weaken with age, and it provides a much smoother power source without the mechanical noise and vibration of a spring. This means that the Sirocco is very smooth to shoot, and can be left cocked for long periods of time with no need to worry about loss of power.

UNDER-LEVERS AND SIDE-LEVERS

Unlike the break-barrel type, underlever and side-lever airguns have a fixed barrel, and you cock them by means of a separate lever which is connected to the piston.

The fixed barrel of these guns has certain advantages. It overcomes the problem of aligning the barrel which I mentioned earlier, and the side-lever in particular can be easier to cock when you are lying down. Many side-lever and underlever guns also have an 'anti-bear trap' mechanism, which stops the lever flying shut if your hand should slip while you are cocking the gun. This can be very dangerous, breaking your fingers if they are in the way, or breaking the gun if they are not! There is no reason in theory why a break-barrel gun could not have an anti-bear trap device, but very few do, probably because the barrel is unikely to trap your hand for the simple reason that it does not shut against anything. It could still damage the gun, however, or trap your fingers in the breech so take care when you are cocking and loading any spring-powered airgun.

Any under-lever or side-lever gun has to have some method of loading the pellet into the breech. This is usually one of two systems – a loading tap or a moving breech which slides back when you cock the gun. The BSA Airsporter has a loading tap, for example, whereas the Weihrauch HW77 has a sliding breech. It is a matter of personal preference which one is the best for you, but if you have large hands you may find the sliding breech type awkward to feed a pellet into. On the other side of the coin, it is possible to leave a pellet sticking out of a loading tap and chop it in half, or even jam the tap.

PNEUMATICS

All of the guns I've described so far suffer from one disadvantage. When you fire, large, heavy metal parts leap about inside the gun, compressing the air in a fraction of a second and squeezing it into the breech. No matter how well the gun is made, and how smoothly the parts move against one another, this causes mechanical noise, and also means that the gun itself jumps *before* the pellet leaves the barrel. Zeroing the sights should take care of any jump which is consistent from one shot to the next, but inevitably it causes some variation between shots and therefore makes the gun less accurate.

The other main group of airguns – the pneumatics – do not suffer from this problem, and are therefore potentially more accurate than any spring and piston airgun.

In a pneumatic, all the effort of compressing the air is done long before the gun is fired. When you pull the trigger, only a tiny part, the valve, moves inside. This releases the air with very little noise, and even less kick – sending the pellet on its way without the gun trying to jump out of alignment.

In practice, however, a good spring airgun is capable of great accuracy despite the mechanical movement of the action, and field target shoots are often won with spring-powered guns against pneumatics.

The main advantage of a pneumatic over a spring airgun is the lack of noise when you fire. Most of the noise from a pneumatic comes from the air 'popping' out of the end of the barrel, and you can reduce this to almost nothing by fitting a silencer. A silencer on a spring airgun will cut down the noise of air leaving the muzzle, but it cannot reduce the mechanical noise of the spring and piston moving in the cylinder so the effect is less impressive.

Pump-up pneumatics

Pneumatics fall into two main types: pump-ups and pre-charged pneumatics. The pump-up type needs to be charged with a built-in pump after each shot, or at least every few shots. This pump is usually situated under the barrel, and the fore-end of the rifle serves as the handle for the pump. The action of pumping the gun is more tiring than cocking a spring-powered weapon, which is the main reason why pump-ups have never really caught on for field target shooting. In a competition you have to shoot a number of targets in quick succession – and pumping the gun after each shot leaves you in no fit state to shoot with the accuracy that you need in order to win.

This type of gun has a pump mechanism rather like a bicycle pump, which compresses the air into a reservoir via a one-way valve. You use a fixed number of pump strokes to reach the same pressure in the reservoir each time. When you pull the trigger, a valve opens and allows the air to rush out of the reservoir into the breech, pushing the pellet down the barrel. This valve is usually the 'dump' type, which means that it opens and stays open, releasing all the air from the reservoir in one go – hence the need to pump the air up again for the next shot. A few pump-ups have a valve which opens for a fraction of a second and then closes again, leaving some compressed air in the reservoir. An example is the Sheridan, which will give you three or four shots from one charging. The problem is that the power falls off drastically from one shot to the next, so you either have to remember three different sets of trajectories, or work out a sequence of pumps and shots to maintain the power for several shots. I owned a Sheridan for a while, and could never get this quite right. It went something like: twelve pumps, fire one shot, four pumps, fire another shot, three pumps, fire the third shot, and so on. Unfortunately, the air temperature and the speed of pumping make a difference, too, so you have to make allowances if you are shooting on a very hot day, and take care to pump at the same speed each time.

Pre-charged pneumatics

The other type of pneumatic is the pre-charged gun, which you charge up well in advance with enough compressed air to fire many shots before the gun needs to be charged again. This avoids the need for tiring pumping between shots, and usually provides more consistent results, although the power begins to drop off after a number of shots have reduced the pressure in the reservoir.

The valve in this type of gun has to be designed carefully so that it releases just the right amount of air when you fire, and closes again immediately to retain the rest of the air in the reservoir. This type of valve normally consists of a valve stem held in the closed position by a spring. When you pull the trigger, a hammer falls on the end of the stem, knocking the valve open for a fraction of a second and allowing a quantity of air to escape before the spring pushes the stem back to the closed position.

A pre-charged pneumatic requires a great deal of highly compressed air to recharge the reservoir. It would be possible to do this with a hand pump, just as shooters in days gone by would have charged up the ball reservoir of an air cane. It would take a lot of pumping, however, and to make life easier for themselves, people nowadays tend to use a cylinder of compressed air similar to those used by deep-sea divers. The cylinder is charged with a compressor driven by a motor, and is then connected up to the airgun's reservoir by a high pressure hose. The high pressure air goes in through a one-way valve, and the gun is ready for use again in a matter of seconds. You can carry the air cylinder in your car, so you have it handy if you need to recharge during a day's shooting.

One interesting development in the area of pre-charged pneumatics is the Sportsmatch GC2, developed by John Ford

This shooter is using a Saxby and Palmer air cartridge rifle. Spare cartridges are kept on a belt, similar to a shotgun cartridge belt.

and Gerald Cardew. This gun has two reservoirs – the main one which is charged from a compressed air cylinder at around 3,000 psi, and a second reservoir which is charged from the first at around 1,500 psi. It is this second reservoir which provides the air to propel the pellet when you pull the trigger. Because it is charged afresh after each shot to the correct pressure, the result is a gun which is very consistent for sixty shots or more, even though the pressure in the first reservoir falls significantly between the first shot and the last.

To my mind, this is the direction in which serious field target and hunting air rifles are going over the next few years. There will always be a place for the robust, reliable, spring-powered airguns, but for those people who insist on superlative performance above all else, the latest pre-charged pneumatics come as close to perfection as anything that man's ingenuity has achieved in the history of airguns. And their other great advantage is their convenience. What could be simpler than charging up your gun at the beginning of the day, and then having nothing more to worry about other than loading a fresh pellet into the breech for each shot? Pre-charged pneumatics tend to be very expensive, as most of them are built by hand in very small numbers. However, as time goes by I expect that they will become more popular and mass production methods will begin to creep in, making them more affordable by the ordinary shooter.

4. The gunmakers

Airgunners, like fishermen, tend to become absorbed in their equipment, and many developments in the history of airguns have come about through keen airgunners experimenting in the pursuit of greater power and accuracy. Sometimes a hobby takes over and becomes a career, for example when an airgunner goes into business tuning other people's guns. Very few airgunners go on to become manufacturers in the true sense, although there are exceptions. To do so requires a great deal more than a knack for airgun design and a lot of enthusiasm. You also must have the financial backing to set up a factory, and the management skills to run a business efficiently and profitably. People who combine all these things are few and far between, with the result that the vast majority of the guns on sale in the shops are made by a relatively small number of manufacturers.

You will often see articles in the airgun magazines debating whether or not foreign gunmakers are superior to those based in Britain. It is true to say that Britain's gunmaking industry is not what it was, but the fact is that there is no need for British shooters to feel ashamed of home manufacturers. Companies such as BSA and Webley make guns which can stand the most critical comparison with foreign weapons, while smaller British companies like Theoben Engineering and Saxby and Palmer are leading the way in modern airgun design.

MASS-PRODUCED GUNS

For sheer value for money, the mass-produced weapons are hard to beat. Companies such as BSA and Webley in this country, and Weihrauch and Original abroad, turn out huge numbers of guns each year. This means that they are buying the basic raw materials in large quantities, and can buy at cheaper prices than you or I could if we went to purchase, for example, a single stock blank. The cost of 'tooling up' a factory is enormous, and if this cost had to be recovered by sales of just a few guns a year, then they would have to be very expensive. Spread over many thousands of guns, this comes down to a much more reasonable level. The result is that the big manufacturers can produce good quality guns which sell at a reasonable price.

It is interesting to look at a mass-produced gun and ask yourself how the various parts have been made. You will find that even the smallest part has been designed to do its job effectively, while being as cheap and simple to manufacture as possible. For a start, the material it is made of will have been chosen with great care. The main working parts must be made of steel to stand up to the forces they will be subjected to, but other parts, such as the sights on some guns, may be made of plastic. Small, intricate parts can be very expensive to make out of metal, when a plastic moulding will do the same job just as well for half the cost. Saving a few pence on a sight may not sound important, but when you apply the same principle to every part of the gun, it can make the difference between success and failure for a manufacturer.

Apart from the material used for the various parts, you will also see that the parts have been designed to be as simple to make as possible. Some of the trigger parts, for example, will probably be pressed out of sheet metal, rather than being cut to shape, drilled and ground. The inside of the stock, where the gun's cylinder fits against the wood, is another place where you can see the short cuts made by mass manufacturers to bring the price down. Very often the wood inside will be roughly finished, and you will be able to see clearly the marks made by the routing machine which gouged out the recess where the action fits.

Most manufacturers make a range of guns rather than just one model, and this is another area where they can save money without detracting from their guns' performance. Instead of designing a completely new gun from scratch, they will try to

The Weihrauch HW77 in its basic form. Compare this with the tuned and customised HW77 shown on page 167.

use the same parts that they are already tooled up to produce. In the BSA range, for example, you will find the same sights, cylinder end blocks, trigger blades, and so on appearing on several different guns across the range. In fact, you can sometimes spot a big manufacturer's parts being used in guns made by smaller manufacturers, because it is cheaper for them to buy the parts than to make them to the same quality themselves. An example of this is the Anschutz barrels and open sights fitted to Theoben air rifles.

So far I have only mentioned ways that manufacturers can keep down their production costs, but of course there is a lot more to it than that. One of their most important activities is marketing – actually selling their products to shooters like you and me. The manufacturer must bear in mind not just the performance of his products, but also their appeal to his customers in the shooting fraternity. A superb looking stock made of polished walnut will not help you put a single bunny in the bag, or knock over another target – but it does make the gun much more attractive to own than one with a tatty looking plastic stock. So the manufacturer must consider not just how his products perform, but also how attractive they are to his customers. Different people want different things, of course, and some are looking for a lot of performance for their money, while others are prepared to pay for a more luxurious looking gun which may not necessarily shoot any better. The result is a rich variety of different guns to choose from, produced by many different manufacturers all over the world.

BRITISH GUNMAKERS

One of the problems that has beset British manufacturing industry over recent years is that the technical and production staff have traditionally ruled the roost. Companies have placed their faith in the old adage 'If you build a better mousetrap, the world will beat a path to your door'. British manufacturers have been justly proud of their products, which are technically among the best in the world. They have tended to lag behind the rest of the world in marketing, however, with the result that foreign competitors have stolen a march on them. In a competitive world, it is not enough to have the best product. You must convince your customers that your product is the best – or the most desirable – through clever advertising and all the other marketing tricks. Design is an important factor, too, and here again foreign manufacturers have been one step ahead of Britain in making their products look more powerful and exciting – even if they are not!

To my mind, British manufacturers lost a lot of ground to the foreign competition, by moaning about how unfair it was that people were ignoring their excellent products while doing nothing to improve their marketing. Things are beginning to look up for Britain, however, as manufacturers wake up to the need for really good marketing as well as technical excellence. Just flip through any of the airgun magazines and you will see how much better British companies have become at selling their wares.

The two main British manufacturers are BSA and Webley, who between them account for a large proportion of the airguns made in this country. Both of these companies make a full range of excellent air rifles and pistols, with something to suit everyone from the complete novice to the serious competitive shooter. But Britain is unique in that it also has a host of smaller companies producing small numbers of highly specialised airguns. Many of these were started by dedicated enthusiasts – people who combined engineering skill with a deep love of airgun shooting. The growth of airgunning as a serious sport in this country has provided them with a ready market for the specialist weapons, which are generally much more expensive and highly finished than the mass-produced guns.

These companies are too numerous to list, but some of the better known are Venom Arms, Theoben Engineering, Daystate, Galway Gun Co, Airmasters and Sportsmatch. It is in companies like these that you will find the real characters of airgun manufacturing – or perhaps building would be a better word – people such as Dave Pope, Ivan Hancock, Ben Taylor, David Theobald and Ken Galway who live, breathe and eat airguns. They may disagree as to which particular design is the best, but they are all working in their own way towards what they believe is the 'ideal' airgun, and they all care passionately about the future of the sport.

Some, like Venom, base their creations on existing weapons. Many of the beautiful custom Venom guns began as very ordinary looking Weihrauch HW80s or HW77s. Once inside the Venom workshops, however, they are stripped down and the process of transforming them into a masterpiece of the gun-smith's art begins. The working parts are honed and polished, some are replaced with specially made parts which will improve the gun's performance still further, and every part is hand-finished to tolerances far closer than the original manufacturer ever contemplated. The external finish receives equally lavish attention, with high quality engraving, gold plating and a stock made specially from selected walnut in one of several configurations intended to give a more comfortable hold and a sleek new look.

Other companies, such as Theoben, take only a few parts from other manufacturers, and create what is essentially a gun of entirely their own design. It is these manufacturers who are really in the business of developing new guns, rather than simply improving on other people's, and it is they who have brought us the innovations of recent years – innovations such as Saxby and Palmer's air cartridge system, Theoben's gas 'spring', and the Sportsmatch twin-reservoir pneumatic.

It is a healthy sign that all these companies are finding a market for their superb weapons, and I find it immensely encouraging that British experts are leading the world in developing the next generation of air weapons. Let's hope that Britain's mass-manufacturers show the same pioneering spirit, and ensure that this country reaps the benefits of these technical developments, rather than seeing them exploited by other countries.

FOREIGN MANU-FACTURERS

Outside Britain, West Germany ranks as one of the major airgun manufacturing countries in the world. Companies such as Weihrauch, Anschutz, RWS, Original and Feinwerkbau spring immediately to mind as leaders in the field. These companies and others like them have become legendary for their superb engineering and high quality guns. Handle a Weihrauch and you will immediately be impressed by the weight and solid feel of the gun. Weihrauch in particular have earned a reputation for powerful, strongly made airguns which are reliable and accurate. The Weihrauch HW35 took the market by storm when it first appeared over a decade ago, and was one of the first of the new generation of airguns which helped the sport to develop into what it is today. Earlier airguns had seemed little more than toys, but here was a gun which offered plenty of power, with the look and feel of a 'real' rifle. The fact that the HW35 is still so popular today, many years on, says a lot for its design, while Weihrauch have continued to develop superb air weapons such as their more recent HW80 and HW77.

Other Western European countries such as Spain have produced some good cheaper guns, such as the Sniper and Paratrooper sold in Britain by ASI, but have never really competed with the Germans at the top end of the market. Another contender in the lower price brackets is Eastern Europe, with guns such as the Relum Tornado from Hungary. Years ago I paid £20 for a second-hand Relum. It was a very basic gun, but had plenty of power and was reasonably accurate. Unfortunately it suffered from a badly worn trigger mechanism, and the trigger pressure needed to fire it varied drastically from one shot to the next. Soon afterwards I bought a BSA Airsporter, and from that time the Relum spent most of its time in the gun cupboard. There are some reasonable East European guns around, however, and they do offer a lot for your money if you are more concerned about performance than finish.

Japan has made far more impact on airgun scopes than on airguns themselves, but one or two good airguns have come out of Japan, notably the pump-up Sharp models. The United States, too, has produced some interesting pump-ups – including the Sheridan – but due to the different guns laws in the States, manufacturers there tend to concentrate on other types of weapon.

5. Custom guns

In the previous chapter we looked at people and companies who actually make airguns, and touched only briefly on the art of converting or 'customising' air weapons. Airgunners tend to be individualists, and are rarely satisfied with a gun off the shelf. They want something a little bit different – a shade more powerful, shaped to fit better, or perhaps embellished with

A gunsmith at work on an airgun stock.

more attractive engravings and fittings. My first air rifle was a BSA Meteor, a good, solid gun capable of reasonable power and accuracy. I spent countless hours in the school holidays plinking at tin cans, matchboxes and any other makeshift target I could find lying around – including the heads of the daffodils in the garden, to my mother's horror! It wasn't long before I became dissatisfied with the little gun, though, and wanted to improve its looks and performance. I couldn't afford to have the work done by an expert, so I set about doing what I could myself. My attempts would look pitiful alongside the work of experts such as Venom, but I gained a great deal of pleasure and learned a lot about how airguns work in the process.

Tuning and customising an airgun is a highly specialised skill, and you can do a lot of harm to a gun if you don't know what you are doing. Some jobs can safely be tackled by an amateur, but if you are at all unsure of yourself it is better to have the work done by an expert rather than risk spoiling a favourite gun.

CUSTOMISING A GUN

The process of customising an airgun falls into two main parts: improving its performance and improving its looks. By performance I mean not just its power, although most custom rifles will have had their power beefed up. The gunsmith will also want to make the rifle shoot more smoothly and accurately than it did off the shelf. The first step is to dismantle the gun completely and polish up all the internal parts to remove the rough edges left by the manufacturing process. Manufacturers simply cannot afford to spend the time necessary to finish the parts by hand, but it can improve the smoothness of the action enormously. Most custom gunsmiths will also alter the mechanism in some way as well, perhaps adding a more powerful spring, or a brass spring guide. Sometimes they will even go so far as to adjust the 'stroke' – the distance the piston travels when you fire. This is done by fitting a new piston of a different length, and perhaps adding or removing shim washers to give the ideal compression ratio.

The transfer port often comes in for special attention. This is the small hole at the end of the cylinder through which the air passes into the breech. A smooth sided, carefully shaped transfer port will allow the air to flow freely, with the minimum of power loss. The trigger mechanism, too, may be polished and altered, but many people prefer to leave the trigger alone, particularly when they are dealing with one of the Weihrauch rifles which are renowned for their excellent Rekord trigger unit.

Weihrauchs are probably the most commonly used as the basis for customs guns, and are highly regarded for their sound basic design and quality of engineering.

The gun's component parts are then reassembled, with great care being taken to lubricate each part properly. Airgun lubrication is an art in itself, and all the more so now that modern silicon based lubricants are available. Some lubrication is essential to allow the various metal parts to slide smoothly over one another, but over-lubrication can be worse than none at all. During my early experiments with my old BSA Meteor, I decided to lubricate the mainspring with tractor grease. I spread the thick, sticky goo all over the spring, spring guide and inside the cylinder, and was seriously disappointed when the gun hardly had the power to push the pellet from the barrel. I spent another couple of hours stripping the gun down again and cleaning off all the grease. Then I sparingly added a couple of drops of light oil, and the result was amazing. The gun had regained its former power, and more. The lesson was clear, and ever since I have been careful not to over-lubricate my guns.

STOCKING AND ENGRAVING

A fine example of a custom stock, showing the thumb-hole grip design and adjustable recoil pad.

Once the custom gunsmith has tuned the mechanics to perfection, he will turn to the external appearance of the gun. This will often involve scrapping the original stock and making a totally new one to a special design from a carefully selected walnut blank. The shape is chosen to fit the shooter more comfortably than a standard stock, and provide a more snug fit to allow him to shoot more accurately. Many custom gunstocks will have an anatomical grip to fit the hand, for instance, perhaps with a thumbhole to allow the hand to find a more comfortable position. There will usually be a raised cheekpiece so that the head is supported in exactly the right position to see

through the scope. Custom guns are almost invariably fitted with a scope, requiring a higher cheekpiece than the standard stock which has to allow for a shooter using either a scope or open sights. A contoured butt-plate will usually be fitted, often adjustable so that the shooter can find the ideal position.

The custom stock will also be finished to a much higher standard than the original, with finely cut chequering or perhaps a stippled grip, and oil polished in the same way as a 'best' English shotgun. The stock may also be decorated with carvings depicting game or shooting scenes, or inlaid with engraved precious metal plates. The most expensive custom guns are made specifically to the owner's requirements, and may include his own name or initials or choice of engravings.

The metal parts of the gun may also be embellished with engraving. Most usually this will be on the cylinder and the blanking plate used to cover the holes left by removing the rearsight from the breech end of the barrel, although sometimes other parts are engraved such as the side face of a one-piece scope mount. Special metal finishes are not often seen, except perhaps gold plating on the trigger blade, but occasionally one comes across a gun which has been extensively gold plated. Not very good camouflage for hunting, perhaps, but a stunning example of the gunmaker's art.

It is rare indeed for one man to possess all the various skills needed to produce a top custom weapon. Individual people tend to specialise in one skill, and the different parts of the gun will probably be handled separately by the craftsmen involved:

High quality engraving on the cylinder of an airgun.

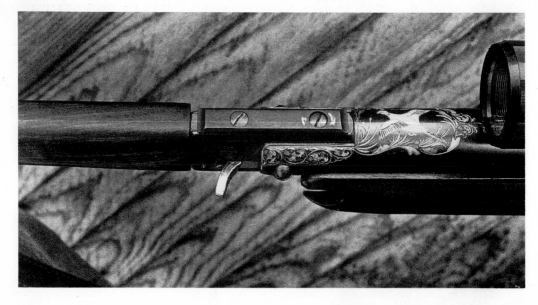

the stock by a stockmaker, the action by a gunsmith specialising in tuning, and the external metal parts by an engraver. The entire gun may be passed from one to another in sequence, or it may be divided into the main parts and these worked on simultaneously by different people. Many of the most skilled crafstmen work from a small workshop at home, and some of the finest custom guns are a product of this sort of cottage industry.

THE COST Such masterpieces don't come cheap, of course. There are many hours of painstaking work involved in turning a standard air rifle into a custom special, not to mention the extra cost of top grade walnut for the stock and any additional materials such as gold for plating. Even a simple tuning will cost from £30 upwards on top of the original price of the gun, and for a really top custom gun you could easily pay in excess of £500.

Beautiful as these custom weapons may be, I prefer my guns to be tools for a job rather than works of art. If I went hunting with a beautifully engraved, highly polished gun, I would be terrified of scratching it, or getting it wet in the long grass. I would rather spend my money on the mechanics of the gun, so that it performed really well, rather than improving its appearance. If you concentrate on field target shooting rather than hunting, however, then your gun is not at such a risk and there is no reason why you should not indulge yourself with a really superb custom weapon. It may even provide some psychological advantage by making your competitors wonder what they are up against when you arrive at the shoot and pull a glittering 'special' out of your guncase!

If you decide to have a go at customising a gun yourself, I would recommend that you concentrate on the woodwork, at least to begin with. You can buy a stock blank and work on it to create a brand new special stock to your own design, oiling and polishing it to give a top quality finish. A new stock will make a dramatic difference to the appearance of the gun, and if the whole operation turns out to be a disaster, then at least you can simply replace the old stock and all you have lost is the cost of the blank. Make a mistake when you are tinkering with the action, and you may have to buy a complete new gun!

6. Power and performance

It might seem surprising when I say that airgunners are inclined to suffer from megalomania, but it is true to say that most of us at some time have been power-mad. We go through a stage when the power of the gun seems all-important, and other aspects of its performance pale into insignificance. This is understandable but unfortunate, because power is actually one of the less important factors in a gun's performance. What is really needed is a balance between power and accuracy. Taking this argument to extremes, one might have a gun which was powerful enough to knock out a tank, but couldn't hit a barn door at twenty paces. Such a gun would be totally useless. After all, if you can't hit the target, any amount of power is no good to you. Even a very weak gun would be better if you could be sure of putting your pellet in the right place every time.

The law in Britain restricts the power of an air rifle to 12 foot pounds at the muzzle. For an air pistol the limit is 6 ft lbs. If you have an airgun that exceeds the legal limit, it is classified as a firearm, and you must have a firearm certificate to own and shoot it. Many airgun manufacturers make a big deal about how powerful their guns are. Just look through any issue of any airgun magazine and you will see advertisements making claims like 'as powerful as the law allows', or 'bang on the legal limit'. Most of these claims are perfectly true – the majority of full-sized air rifles do provide around 12 ft lbs at the muzzle. What the advertisements don't tell you, though, is how consistent and accurate the guns are. A gun may be producing an *average* of 12 ft lbs, but if every third shot comes out at 10.5 ft lbs, then you will not be able to shoot consistently with it. So don't dismiss the manufacturers' claims entirely. They are simply doing their job in trying to sell airguns. But do bear in mind that there is much more to choosing an air rifle than just picking the most powerful one. A 10 ft lb airgun is quite powerful enough to kill a rabbit, or knock over a field target – if you can consistently put the pellet in the right place.

MEASURING POWER

The power of the airgun is actually a measure of energy, kinetic energy to be precise. It is a function of the pellet's mass (or weight), and its velocity. If you take a gun producing 12 ft lbs, it might fire a very heavy pellet relatively slowly, or a light pellet at a higher velocity. The difference comes further on in the pellet's flight, because a heavy pellet retains its energy longer in the face of air resistance or 'drag'. This is worth remembering when you choose a pellet, because it is the energy of the pellet when it hits the target that counts, not at the muzzle.

Energy is rather difficult to measure, and it is a lot simpler to measure the velocity of the pellet as it leaves the muzzle. This is done with the aid of a device known as a chronograph. Chronographs come in different shapes and sizes, but most of them work on the same principle. There are two photo-electric cells which 'see' the shadow of the pellet as it passes over them. The cells are fixed at a measured distance apart, and the electronic circuitry inside the machine registers the time the pellet takes to pass from one cell to the next. It then converts this time into velocity in feet or metres per second. Provided you know the weight of the pellet, you can then work out the kinetic energy by substituting the values you have obtained into a relatively simple equation:

$$\text{Energy (ft lbs)} = \frac{\text{Velocity (feet per sec)}^2 \times \text{Pellet weight (grains)}}{450,240}$$

A chronograph is quite an expensive piece of equipment and few shooters buy one for themselves. It can be very helpful, though, particularly if you like tinkering with your gun to improve its performance, or if you enter field target shoots and need to check that your gun will pass the chronograph test before you enter. You may be able to club together with friends and buy a chronograph between you. Don't forget that you will also need to know the weight of your usual pellets. The weight might vary slightly from one batch to another, but not normally enough to make a significant difference to the calculation. You can look up the weight of different pellets in tables printed every now and again in the airgun magazines, or find a friendly pharmacist who will use his special scales. If you cannot find a set of scales accurate enough to weigh a single pellet, you can weigh a number and divide the result to give the weight of a single pellet. This will give you an average weight for all the pellets included in the sample. As a guide, Eley's popular Wasp pellets weigh 7.40 grains in .177, and 14.50 grains in .22 calibre.

ACCURACY

More important than power, to my mind, is the consistency and accuracy of an air rifle. Part of the reason for tuning an air rifle is often to increase its power, but with a rifle such as the Weihrauch HW80, the power is probably right on the legal limit before you take it out of the box. Careful tuning will leave it within the legal limit, but will make the gun much more consistent by removing the variability between shots that is caused by slight irregularities in the piston and cylinder, for example. Doing this will help you to shoot tighter groups, which is what accuracy is all about. It is all very well to be able to put a single pellet through the bullseye, but the real skill comes in putting the next pellet, and the next, through the same hole. The smoothness of the action makes a big difference to how consistently you can shoot a gun. I mentioned in a previous chapter that in a spring air rifle, all the mechanical movement in the action happens before the pellet has left the muzzle. This movement can easily upset the pellet's flight, particularly if it sets up vibrations which are transmitted to the barrel. One useful test is to listen to the gun fire, which is most easily done if someone else is firing it. Listen out for harsh, metallic vibrations which indicate that the action is not running smoothly. Shooting a group on a paper target will also be a useful guide, but you must make allowances for your own shooting skill. The best way to test the rifle's potential for shooting an accurate group is to fire a group from a bench rest, which ensures that the barrel is pointing in exactly the same direction for each shot. A bench rest can mask the effects of vibration, however, which only become apparent when the gun is held by a human shooter. After all, no one can hold a gun as firmly as a good bench rest – and you don't take a bench rest with you when you go shooting.

Proper lubrication also plays an important part in getting the best performance from a gun. The best advice anyone can give on lubricating an air rifle is to go easy. It's very easy to over-lubricate, but very few people under-lubricate their airguns. The vital point is never to put any lubricant in front of the piston, otherwise you are asking for trouble. Even the tiniest drop of oil in front of the piston will become vaporised by the first shot, and the next shot is likely to cause the gun to diesel, with potentially serious results. Don't be tempted to make your gun diesel deliberately. Not only is it illegal, because the gun will be shooting way above the legal power limit, but the high pressures created in the cylinder can easily damage it.

7. Safety

Warning: airguns can kill. That may sound rather strong, but it is perfectly true that a modern airgun is capable of killing a human being. An airgun may not be as powerful as a cartridge rifle or shotgun, but a hit in the head or heart can be lethal – and a pellet can inflict a nasty injury on any part of the body. There are many well-documented cases of people being killed or maimed with airguns, and you would do well to remember that if you are ever tempted to take a risk. I have come across two cases of injuries caused by air rifles, although thankfully no permanent damage was done. In each case, the accident was entirely avoidable, and happened because the people involved ignored the risks and flouted the basic rules of gun safety. Accidents will happen – but only if you let them.

I have also witnessed some quite astonishingly stupid behaviour with airguns which by sheer good fortune have not resulted in an accident, but could easily have done so. A friend who visited my house once asked if he could try a few shots with my air rifle, and assured me that he had used one before and knew the rules. I turned my back for a second, and was amazed to see him peering down the muzzle of the loaded gun to see if there was an obstruction in the barrel! I shudder to think what would have happened if the gun had gone off accidentally when he knocked the butt on the ground.

I doubt that many people would do anything quite so stupid as that, but there are less obvious ways in which you can put yourself or others in danger without realising it.

SAFETY RULES

The first rule of gun safety is never to point the gun at anyone, or anything, that you don't wish to shoot. There are no exceptions to this rule, even when the gun is unloaded. If you are carrying the gun, hold it in a safe position so that even if it should discharge accidentally, the pellet will do no damage. Many people carry their guns over their shoulder, with the barrel pointing at the sky, but you should bear in mind that what goes up must come down – and the pellet will fall to earth somewhere.

It is also all too easy to let the barrel droop when your arm tires, so that it is actually pointing parallel to the ground. The safest method, in my opinion, is to rest the gun in the crook of your elbow, with the muzzle pointing at the ground. Better still, keep the gun unloaded when you are walking, and only load when you are close to taking a shot. You should always unload when you have to cross any obstacle, such as climbing a fence or crawling through a hedge. Far too many accidents have happened when someone has left his gun on the other side of a hedge, and then reached back to pull the gun through by the barrel. The trigger catches on a twig, and the gun goes off. Certainly, you should always unload when you are standing around talking to other people. When you are in company, it is a good idea not just to be safe, but to be seen to be safe. This means breaking the gun if it is a break-barrel airgun, or leaving the bolt open. That way everyone around you can see that the gun is unloaded, and they will feel a lot more comfortable.

Another rule to follow is don't shoot where you cannot see. That may sound obvious, but what about that pigeon sitting in a bush on the edge of the wood? Where will the pellet go if you miss? Into the wood of course – and can you be sure that there isn't someone having a picnic on the far side? No, you can't, and don't be tempted to think it cannot happen, because it can – all too easily. Every time you take a shot, you should ask yourself where the pellet could end up, and that applies whether you are hunting or just practising in the garden. Remember, too, that a pellet can easily ricochet off a hard surface, or even water or rubber such as an old car tyre. I once fired at an old tyre in a farmyard, and was amazed to hear the pellet zip past my ear a second later. It hit the barn behind me with enough force to embed itself in the weatherboarding, so it still had enough energy left to do some damage if it had hit me. In the field, the only safe background is solid earth, and if you are shooting up into the air – at a pigeon in a tree, for instance – then you will need several hundred yards of clear space behind the target to be sure of a safe shot. For practising in the garden, it is a good idea to build a safe backstop to place behind the target. This should be large enough to be sure of catching any stray pellets – at least three or four feet across – and it should consist of good solid backing covered with something which will absorb the pellets' energy, such as a piece of old carpet.

I have already mentioned that you should always unload your rifle whenever you are in company, and the same applies when you put the gun down for any reason, even for a moment. Very often, the easiest way to do this is to fire it off into soft earth, because it can be difficult to extract a pellet from the breech. You should never assume that others are as careful as you, though. Even the most conscientious people can make mistakes, and it only takes a moment to check that a gun is unloaded when you pick it up or take it from someone else. It is a good habit to get into. I have only once found a gun loaded in the hundreds or even thousands of times that I have checked a gun when I picked it up. But if I had forgotten that one time, who knows what might have happened?

THE SAFETY CATCH

Some airguns are fitted with a device called a safety catch. Don't be fooled. Pushing a button from 'off' to 'on' does not make a gun safe. Far from it. In fact, it can make it less safe because with the safety catch on you may be tempted to treat the gun as if it were unloaded. In most guns, the safety catch simply blocks the trigger blade so that it cannot move. Therefore you can't fire the gun by pulling the trigger – but the spring is still compressed, the pellet still in the breech. If the sear slips, the gun will fire – and it can be surprisingly easy to make a gun fire without pulling the trigger, by knocking the butt on the ground, for instance. So never use a safety catch as a lazy way of immobilising the gun when you cross a fence or stop to chat to someone. If the gun needs to be made safe, you must unload it. By all means use the safety catch while you are stalking to prevent you pulling the trigger accidentally, but treat the gun with the same respect whether the catch is on or off.

THE SPRING

So much for the dangers of a loaded airgun, or one which appears to be unloaded but isn't. But there are other dangers involved in using airguns, particularly when you are cocking them or dismantling them. The trouble is that an airgun contains a very powerful spring, which is compressed even when the gun is uncocked. If you release that pressure without controlling it, then watch out! The two most obvious examples are when you are cocking a gun and your hand slips, or when you remove the pin which retains the mainspring while you are stripping the gun.

The old Relum Tornado that I described earlier had a separate cocking lever under the barrel, which took a considerable amount of effort to pull all the way back until the sear engaged. Even then, the trigger mechanism sometimes failed, allowing all the spring's force to snap the cocking lever back suddenly against the barrel – very much like the jaws of a trap. I was aware of the danger, and always took great care to keep my hands clear, but a friend who borrowed the gun once received a nasty bruise. He was lucky not to break his fingers, and I felt guilty for not warning him clearly enough about the gun's unpredictable trigger. Some airguns have a ratchet known as an anti-bear trap device, which prevents the cocking lever from slamming closed part-way through the cocking stroke. Some of these will still allow it to slam shut once the sear has engaged, however, so you must still take care and not be lulled into a false sense of security. I will always remember what the Red Devils' instructor told me shortly before my first – and last – parachute jump: 'Any mechanical device can fail, and you would do well to assume that it will do just that, at the worst possible moment'. In the event, the parachute worked perfectly, but I landed awkwardly and broke my ankle!

The gun's breech is another potential trap for unwary fingers. Normally, you will cock the gun, bringing the cocking lever or barrel back to its original position, and then place a pellet in the breech. In doing so, you must insert your fingers between two pieces of metal which are held open only by the sear of the trigger, while all the power of the spring tries to slam them together. It is sensible to keep your fingers out of the breech area as much as possible, and keep your other hand well away from the trigger. Tap-loading rifles avoid this risk altogether, while I have always felt that the breech of the Weihrauch HW77 is particularly badly designed from this point of view.

Many people do not realise that the spring in most airguns is held under compression even when it is uncocked. If it wasn't, it would rattle around inside the gun. This means you must be very careful when you dismantle the gun for any reason, such as to replace the mainspring. A gunsmith will use a special tool known as a spring compressor, which allows him to compress the spring slightly and relieve the pressure on the pin which holds it in place. Then he can release the spring's pressure slowly and safely. You may be able to make your own spring compressor from an old sash cramp or similar, and this would be a good idea if you spend much time tinkering with your guns since it would save a great deal of time and temper. Without a spring compressor, it is best to ask someone to help you remove the spring and, even more tricky, to replace it again.

PNEUMATICS

Pneumatic airguns have no mainspring to cause you problems, of course, but they do present a new set of dangers. The high pressures needed to propel a pellet are sufficient to do considerable damage if, for example, the reservoir containing the compressed air burst open. Normally, this is very unlikely to happen. Pneumatic airguns are very well made, and tested to much higher pressures than they will ever have to stand in normal use. The danger comes when you decide to mess around with the gun to increase its power. Many pneumatic guns have a let-off valve which releases the air if the pressure in the reservoir becomes too great. It might be tempting to block this valve and try to put a couple of extra pumps in to give a higher muzzle energy: don't! The valve is there for a very good reason. It protects the reservoir against pressures which could cause it to burst, and it also ensures that the gun cannot be pumped up beyond the legal power limit. By blocking it, you not only break the law, but you also run a very real risk of being injured by shrapnel when the reservoir bursts. High pressures can also damage the main valve which fires the gun, or even jam it solid so that the gun will not fire at all.

All these safety precautions really boil down to one word: respect. You should respect your gun, and what it is capable of doing. Most accidents happen because someone didn't stop to think about the consequences. With a reasonable amount of care, you can enjoy a lifetime of safe shooting, without endangering yourself or anyone else. It only takes a moment to check whether a gun is loaded, but forget and you could spend the rest of your life regretting it.

LEAD PELLETS

There is one final aspect of safety that needs to be mentioned in the context of airgun shooting. Most airgun pellets are made of lead, a metal which is known to be poisonous. Small amounts of lead can build up in the body over a period of time, eventually causing unpleasant symptoms. You should therefore avoid getting lead from your pellets into your mouth, either directly by holding pellets in your mouth or indirectly via your fingers. Don't store pellets loose in your pocket, because the lead will rub off on the inside of your pocket and could later be transferred into your mouth. For the same reason, you should wash your hands after handling pellets, and before you eat, smoke or drink. Pellets should not be left lying around the house, where your children or pets might pick them up.

8. Looking after your airgun

Even the cheapest airgun will give you years of service if you look after it properly. On the other hand, you might spend a small fortune on a top quality gun, only to have it rust solid through neglect in just a few weeks. In fact, most airgunners begin by lavishing too much care on their guns rather than too little. When you buy a new gun, it's tempting to spend hours polishing and oiling it, which can actually do more harm than good. An airgun should be kept clean, free from rust, and lubricated just enough so that there is not excessive wear on the mechanical parts.

When you buy a new airgun it may be wrapped in greased paper to prevent it rusting while on the gunsmith's shelves. Remove the paper, and wipe off any excess grease, which could attract grit. Rub all the external metal parts with a lightly oiled cloth to leave a thin film of oil, but don't touch the inside of the gun. The manufacturer will have lubricated the mechanism properly before the gun left the factory.

AT THE END OF THE DAY

After every day's shooting, you should clean and oil the gun before putting it away. Moisture is the gun's worst enemy, and will soon cause it to rust, spoiling its looks and performance. If you and your gun are caught in a downpour, you will need to strip it down and wipe off any damp that has penetrated inside. Water can find its way quite easily into the gap between the woodwork and the action, so pay special attention to this area. Check over the entire gun for spots of blood, mud and so on, and make sure that all this is removed. An old toothbrush is handy for cleaning dirt out of the chequering, and in awkward corners such as around the breech. Once you have cleaned off all moisture and dirt, give the metal a wipe with a lightly oiled rag. Nowadays there are specially developed oils for protecting the metal parts from rust. These usually come in the form of an aerosol, which you spray onto the surface. The light oil soon dries, leaving an invisible protective coating on the metal. Take care not to leave fingerprints on the surface, as these contain moisture which can cause rust. It is best to store guns in a warm, airy place. Beware of cold, damp places such as cellars, and don't keep a gun where condensation might form. You are unlikely to store your guns in the kitchen or bathroom, but a utility room with a washing machine can also suffer from condensation. The best place is probably a cupboard in your bedroom, and if it is under lock and key, so much the better.

STRIPPING DOWN

For most of the time, this is all the attention your gun will need to keep it working at its best. From time to time, though, it is a good idea to give it a thorough overhaul, and re-lubricate the internal parts. To do this, begin by removing the stock from the action. This will normally be held in place by two or three screws, which should come out quite easily with a screwdriver.

Some examples of the range of different gun maintenance products available – shown here with two cartridge pistols rather than airguns.

Next remove the mainspring and piston, taking care that the mainspring does not fly out and hurt you. You may have to remove the trigger unit before you can take out the piston, or perhaps pull the trigger so that the sear does not catch the piston as you remove it from the cylinder. You will probably also have to disconnect the cocking linkage. Check in your gun's instruction manual for details of how to strip it down, and place

all the screws, washers and other small parts in a container as you go along so that they won't get lost.

Then wipe off any old lubricant, which will contain small particles of metal and dirt. After a while this mixture of oil and dirt becomes abrasive, like grinding paste, and can cause undue wear. Then re-lubricate everything with a small amount of light oil before putting the gun back together. I emphasise the need to use only a small amount of oil. Too much will simply splash about inside the gun, and eventually find its way into the wood of the stock, where it can cause damage. One important point to remember is that you shouldn't put any lubricant in front of the piston, otherwise the gun could diesel. Rest assured that sufficient oil will find its way in front of the piston seal to lubricate it and prevent corrosion. While the gun is dismantled, it is worthwhile checking the piston seal for damage. If it is not perfectly round, it is time to replace it with a new one. Modern silicon-based lubricants provide an alternative to the old-fashioned mineral oils, and are less prone to cause dieselling. They are generally more expensive than traditional oils, but a small tin will last a long time if you use it properly, and in my opinion it is well worth the small extra cost. When you reassemble the gun, add a drop of a proprietary locking compound on the thread of any screw which has shown a tendency to work loose. This will keep it in place until you next want to strip the gun down.

It is a good idea to make a habit of regularly checking the gun for wear or damage, paying particular attention to parts which are likely to wear out, such as breech sealing rings. You can buy replacement parts quite cheaply, and it's usually a simple matter to fit them yourself.

The bore of the rifle is one part which is usually best left alone. Unlike a cartridge rifle or shotgun, an airgun produces no deposits of burnt powder which could cause corrosion, and each pellet that you fire clears any foreign matter from the barrel. Some airgunners buy small felt discs which they fire like pellets to clean the bore, finishing up with one soaked in oil to leave a protective coating on the rifling. This may be a good idea if you are going to leave the gun unused for some time, but I have never felt the need with guns that are in regular use.

If you do allow rust to form on the exterior of the gun, you will have to remove it with wire wool or a similar abrasive, otherwise it will continue to eat into the metal, causing deep pitting. Don't use sandpaper, as this can cause scratches which will be difficult to remove. You will find that removing the rust will also take off the blueing from the surface, leaving the shiny metal underneath. Blueing is a form of oxidation, and it is carried out in large vats containing a cocktail of rather unpleasant chemicals – not a job you can do at home! You can buy small pots of gun blueing paste or cream for touching up small areas, but the result is not as good as a professional job. If the blueing becomes badly worn over a large area, you may prefer to take the gun to a gunsmith for a complete re-blueing. This is not cheap, however, so be warned!

LOOKING AFTER THE STOCK

The woodwork of the stock requires some attention, too, to keep it looking its best. Most of the cheaper airguns have beech stocks covered with a polyurethane varnish, which has a shiny appearance. This is quite tough, and protects the wood from damp, but it can quickly become chipped and scratched and begin to look tatty. You can touch up any chips and the deeper scratches as they occur, but the only way to restore the stock to its original looks is to strip off the old varnish and apply a new finish. If you are going to all this trouble, you may well decide to use an oil finish, rather than cover the wood again with varnish. To remove the old varnish, use a proprietary varnish remover, following the instructions on the can. Then rub the stock down well with fine sandpaper to smooth out any irregularities and provide a good base for the new finish. That is easy to write, but it takes a lot of time and elbow grease, so don't start unless you're determined to see the job through. When you're applying new varnish, use several thin coats, and rub the surface with sandpaper once one coat is dry before applying the next.

An oil-finished stock is not so shiny as a varnished one, and it will take a lot more punishment before its looks begin to suffer. This is the type of finish used on the stocks of 'best' English shotguns. Usually all you will need to do is treat any dents and scratches, and it won't be necessary to re-finish the entire stock. Dents can be removed by raising them with steam. You will have to hold the affected part of the stock over the spout of a boiling kettle, or rig up a device which will produce a small jet of steam that you can play over the dent. The steam will make the wood swell, and you must then rub down the raised area with sandpaper to make it smooth and flush with the rest of the stock. Finally, you will need to replace the oil which has been removed in the process. You can buy kits containing all the bits and pieces you will need, together with a specially blended stock finishing oil which has to be rubbed in with a soft cloth.

SCOPE MAINTENANCE

Finally on the subject of maintenance, if your gun is fitted with a scope this will need some attention too. Normally all you need do is wipe the surface to remove any damp or dirt. Use the lens caps to keep water and dust off the lenses as much as possible, and remember to fit the caps when the gun is stored. If you do get any drops of water or dust on the lens, dab them off with a soft tissue. Do not rub the lens surface, because you can easily damage the coating. You should never try to dismantle a scope, because not only will this invalidate the guarantee, but you can very easily break the delicate reticule inside. You will also allow moist air into the scope, which can cause problems with condensation later. If the scope fails to work properly for any reason, take it back to the dealer you bought it from.

All in all, looking after an air rifle does not involve much time or trouble, and costs virtually nothing. Failing to maintain it properly can be very expensive, not to mention the heartbreaking experience of opening the cupboard to find your pride and joy covered in a thin film of brown rust. A few minutes with an oily rag at the end of a day's shooting will be time well spent.

9. Airgun calibres

One decision that you will have to make when you buy an airgun, once you have settled on the make and model, is its calibre. Most airguns are available in either .177 or .22 calibre, but you may also be offered .20 or .25. What do these figures mean, and how should you go about choosing which one is best for your needs?

Airgun calibres are nearly always given in inches, so .22 means that the bore of the barrel measures 22 hundredths of an inch across. On the Continent, these calibres are sometimes referred to in millimetres, so .22 becomes 5.5mm. Just to make things more complicated, British .22 air rifles actually have a bore of 5.6mm, with the result that British .22 guns usually perform best with British pellets, and Continental guns with Continental pellets.

The .22 and .177 calibres have for a long time been the most popular, with .22 being regarded as the calibre for serious hunting, and .177 for target shooting. The other two calibres, .20 and .25, have enjoyed something of a revival recently, but they still are nowhere near as popular as the others. The .177 pellet is relatively small and light, and therefore follows a flatter trajectory than the larger .22. This makes it more suitable for target shooting, especially where the range of the target may vary, as in field target competitions. In paper target competitions, the .177 pellet punches a smaller hole, making scoring easier. And as an extra bonus, .177 pellets are cheaper than .22.

THE CALIBRE CONTROVERSY

People used to believe that the .177 calibre was too small for hunting. They felt that the .177 pellet would not have the stopping power necessary to give a clean kill against a live target such as a rabbit. These ideas were based in the days when .177 airguns were weak target shooting guns, but as more powerful airguns developed, .177 gained a following which advocated its use for hunting. The 'calibre controversy', as it became known, raged in the airgun magazines, with fans of both calibres battling it out on the letters pages.

The argument went something like this: suppose you took a powerful hunting rifle – the Weihrauch HW35 was one of the most popular at the time – which was available in .177 or .22 calibre. The only difference between the two guns was the barrel, which was fitted to an identical action. A pellet fired from the .177 version would have the same muzzle energy as one fired from the .22, but because of the difference in the pellets' weight, the .177 pellet would have a greater velocity. This velocity gave it a flatter trajectory, which its fans said gave it the advantage because it was easier to shoot accurately at unpredictable ranges in the field. You would need less holdover at a given range, and if you estimated incorrectly, you would miss the mark by a smaller amount. True enough, said the .22 camp, but what happens when the pellet strikes its target? The .177 pellet may have the same energy, but it doesn't have the stopping power of a larger pellet.

STOPPING POWER

Stopping power is a difficult thing to measure. It is the capacity of the pellet to inflict sufficient damage on a live target to kill it instantly, and it depends not only on the degree of damage inflicted but also the shock effect of the pellet striking. Those in favour of the .22 argued that the larger pellet had a larger shock effect, making it more likely to stop the target in its tracks. To support their argument, they conducted experiments on terminal ballistics using ballistic putty, a substance which is used to test the effect of projectiles on live targets. The putty is formed into a block, and a pellet fired into it. The block is then cut in half, and the hole made by the pellet is studied. A .22 pellet penetrates less far into the block, but makes a hole with a much larger diameter – showing that the shock of impact is greater.

All very well, said the .177 fans, but the tests did not take account of penetration. The .177 pellet would penetrate better through layers of feathers on a pigeon, for example, and would travel further through an animal's body – making it more likely to hit a vital organ and kill instantly.

One cannot humanely conduct experiments to test stopping power, of course. When you shoot at live quarry, your objective must be to kill it as quickly and painlessly as possible. There can be no justification for prolonging its suffering in the interests of science. Some airgunners did try to resolve the issue by keeping detailed records of every shot they took at live quarry, dissecting their bag and making notes on the effect of many dozens of shots.

It was suggested that different calibres were best for different quarry. The .22 was recommended for ground game such as rabbits, while .177 was supposed to be better for pigeons because it would penetrate their tough feathers more effectively. '.22 for fur, .177 for feather' became the common theme.

In the midst of all this argument, there were those who preferred the 'oddball' calibres of .20 and .25. The .20 calibre was suggested as a compromise between .177 and .22, since it falls roughly mid-way between them in size. It was said that .20 offered the best of both worlds, giving a reasonably fast velocity and therefore acceptably flat trajectory with good penetration, and yet still having sufficient shock effect for a clean kill. Fans of the .25 calibre took the view that shock effect was everything. You might miss the occasional target with .25 due to its more curved trajectory, they said, but if you scored a hit the result was in no doubt. The massive .25 pellet would have a devastating effect on the quarry. Nowadays the heat has gone out of the calibre controversy somewhat. The big, heavy .25 calibre still has a few fans, but they are very restricted in the guns and pellets they can choose from. A few people use .25 specifically for certain quarry – particularly rats. There are also relatively few guns and pellets available in .20 calibre, although this calibre too still has a number of fans.

The .177 calibre has become the standard for field target shooting. It has sufficient power to knock over the most distant field target, and its flat trajectory gives a definite advantage in the precise discipline of target competition. Target shooters who also go hunting tend to stick with their favourite calibre for live quarry, too, and their results speak for themselves.

The .22 calibre refuses to go away, however, and still has a loyal following. Personally, I cannot see that the calibre controversy will ever be resolved. It is difficult to see how the arguments can be proved one way or the other. Each shot is an individual case, and who can know what might have happened if you had been using a different calibre? I believe that the important thing is not to worry too much about the calibre. The fact is that if you hit your quarry in the right spot, you will kill it instantly regardless of whether you are using .177, .20, .22 or even .25. Select the calibre you feel most happy with, and then concentrate on shooting accurately. If things start to go wrong for you, there are a hundred and one things that you should consider before worrying about whether you should change to a different calibre. It's far more likely that your shooting position is wrong, or you are snatching at the trigger.

10. Ammunition

Even when you have selected the calibre of your airgun, the choice is not over. In fact it is only just beginning, because there are many different types of pellet in the two main calibres, and even in .20 you can choose between several varieties of pellet.

Most airgun pellets are made of lead, although there are a few exceptions, as we will see later. Lead is a good material for a pellet: it is very dense, so even a small pellet such as a .177 is relatively heavy and will have the energy to force its way to the target against air resistance. Imagine a pellet made of polystyrene. It would fall to the ground a foot or two from the muzzle, because it is far too light. Lead can also be melted down and cast into pellet shapes, making it easy to manufacture. Being a relatively soft metal, it is forced by the air to fit the shape of the bore, gripping the rifling and sealing the bore so that air does not escape past it. Lead also has one or two disadvantages. Because it is soft, the pellets can easily become deformed, which will affect their accuracy. And it is also toxic, so you must take care not to get it in your mouth. If you skipped the earlier chapter on safety, now is the time to look back and see what precautions to take with lead pellets.

THE DIABOLO PELLET

Years ago most airguns fired round balls of lead. There are still a few BB guns around today which use small round pellets, but nearly all modern pellets follow the familiar diabolo shape. This consists of a head which fits neatly into the bore of the gun, a narrow waist, and a broader skirt which is just too big to fit the bore. The skirt expands when the gun is fired, sealing the bore and gripping the rifling tightly. The diabolo shape is aerodynamically very stable, and helps the pellet to fly straight and true. It also reduces friction in the bore, because the pellet only touches the sides of the barrel at two points: the widest part of the head, and the end of the skirt.

There are many different makes and styles of pellet, but they fall into a small number of basic types. The most familiar type is the roundhead which as the name suggests has a rounded head.

This is a good all-purpose pellet, which performs well for hunting, target shooting and practice. Perhaps the best-known example is the Eley Wasp, which follows the classic roundhead pattern with a ribbed skirt.

Another type is the flathead or wadcutter pellet. This was originally designed for target shooting, because the flat head punches a neat, round hole in a paper target, making it easier to work out the score. The flat head has another effect, too. It gives a larger shock effect against a live target, making the flathead pellet a popular choice for shooting live quarry – especially with .177 calibre, when the shock effect may be lacking with a smaller pellet. It might look as though the flathead pellet is not very aerodynamic, but in practice it performs very well and can give great accuracy.

Another design, which was developed specially for shooting live quarry, is the hollow point. This has a concave head, similar to the dum-dum bullets sometimes used in cartridge weapons. The idea is that the pellet will expand on impact, causing greater damage and increasing the shock effect. In fact, an airgun pellet does not have anywhere near the same energy as a bullet from a cartridge rifle or pistol, and even a hollow point pellet does not expand significantly when it hits the target. The shape may increase the shock effect slightly, but it is unlikely to be any greater than a flathead.

Following the opposite line of thought, the pointed pellet was developed to give maximum penetration. This design became popular around the time that people were debating which calibre was best for different quarries, and it was promoted as an answer to lack of penetration with .22 calibre. The sharply pointed head was supposed to help the pellet penetrate the tough outer feathers of a pigeon, and some people claimed to have increased their success rate considerably by using pointed pellets for hunting.

There are a few variations on these basic designs. The Silver Jet pellet, for example, has three rings around the head, all of which fit neatly in the bore of the gun. These rings are intended to increase the pellet's stability in the barrel, and block any air which might leak around the skirt.

AIRGUN 'BULLETS'

One very different type of pellet is more of a bullet than a pellet in shape. Sold under the name of NATO Bullets, these pellets are extremely heavy, and are intended for firearm certificate air rifles well over the 12 ft lbs limit. I have not tried them, but they are claimed to be very effective for hunting, with tremendous stopping power.

I have, however, used a similar type of pellet which was also bullet-shaped, but which you had to make yourself by moulding it from molten lead. A friend bought a .22 calibre pellet mould, and we managed to scrounge some scrap lead which we melted down on the kitchen stove. Using a teaspoon fitted with a makeshift wooden handle, we poured a few drops of molten lead into the mould, then opened it up and tapped the shiny new pellets out to cool. Once they were cool enough to handle, we trimmed off the little tails formed by the hole through which the molten lead was poured. These pellets were rather disappointing in use, although making them was almost a sport in itself. They were far too heavy for the guns that we had available, so their trajectory was very curved and it was difficult to mould them consistently enough, with the result that their accuracy wasn't what it might have been. When we did manage to hit the target, though, there was no doubting their stopping power. The heavy lead slug would stop a rat or rabbit in its tracks.

ALTERNATIVES TO LEAD

There have been a few attempts to use alternative materials for airgun pellets as a way of getting round some of the disadvantages of lead. The first one that I came across was the Prometheus, a pellet made from steel and plastic. A steel shaft formed the core of the pellet, with a rounded nose. The steel stem fitted into a plastic outer shaped like a cotton reel with a hole down the centre. The idea was that the steel centre provided the weight and penetrating power of the pellet, while the softer plastic would seal the bore and engage the rifling. These pellets ran into the problem that field target competition rules specified that lead pellets had to be used, although they have a loyal following among hunters, and a new improved version has recently been launched.

An even more innovative idea enjoyed a brief rise to fame a few years ago. Called Sabo, it was a two-piece pellet consisting of a bullet shaped metal core and a plastic sabot which you had to place around the bullet before loading it into the barrel. When you fired, the sabot fell away a few feet beyond the muzzle, leaving the pellet to continue on its way. The Sabo could not be used with a silencer, because the plastic sabot would have jammed inside. Loading the pellets into the breech could be fiddly, and you needed a special dispenser to do the job properly. I still have a couple of boxes of these pellets in my gun cupboard, but I have not seen them advertised recently.

ACCURACY OF PELLETS

The precise shape of the pellet is a matter for personal choice, and at the end of the day it probably makes no difference to your score, or the size of your bag. Much more important, to my mind, is the quality and consistency of your pellets. The key factor in accurate shooting is that you must be able to shoot consistently. It is no good being able to hit the target once in every three shots. Every shot should go in the same place – and you cannot achieve that if your pellets vary in weight or shape from one to the next.

Airgun pellets are manufactured to set tolerances, like anything else. The manufacturer must accept that each pellet will vary slightly from the next. But he may allow a wide variation, or may be very particular, rejecting any pellets which do not come very close to the specified size, shape and weight. Likewise, some manufacturers will take more trouble than others in selecting their raw materials, and setting up the machines which form the pellets. The result of all this is that some pellets are more consistent than others – and in general the more consistent ones are more expensive. I have always believed that it is worth spending that little bit extra for pellets which are of better quality and more consistent. You may not shoot any better, but at least that is one less thing to blame for your mistakes!

Some shooters use a device called a pellet sizer to ensure that all their pellets are exactly the same diameter at the skirt. You insert the pellet into a hole in the pellet sizer, and push it through with a plunger. This takes time, because you must size each pellet individually, but many people believe that they shoot more accurately as a result. A similar idea is to use a pellet pusher to push each pellet the same distance into the breech of the gun. You can buy specially made pellet pushers, but the end of a biro does the trick just as well. Once again, it takes more time, but seating the pellet nicely into the rifling may give a more consistent result.

If you are really concerned about the quality of your pellets, you can buy match pellets which are made to very high standards, and packed individually so that they cannot be damaged by knocking against each other in a tin. It is even possible to buy packs of pellets which have been individually picked and checked by hand, and are guaranteed to be totally consistent. This is probably going to extremes for most of us, but if you are competing at the highest level you may feel it is worth the extra expense to be absolutely sure that your pellets won't let you down.

**LOOKING AFTER
YOUR PELLETS**

Whatever pellets you choose, it makes sense to look after them properly and avoid damaging them. When I buy a tin of pellets, I tip them out and check them over for any mis-shapen ones, which I throw away. I also get rid of any loose bits of metal in the tin, which could stick to a pellet and affect its flight. A tin is usually rather inconvenient to carry around, so I transfer a small number into a smaller container which will protect them – the plastic containers that 35mm film is sold in are quite useful. Don't carry pellets loose in your pocket, or let them roll around the car, because they will quickly become dented and mis-shapen, and will not be so accurate. You should also be careful not to damage the pellet when you insert it into the breech. It is all too easy to leave it sticking out slightly, and dent the skirt when you close the breech – particularly with a tap-loading rifle. Once you have done this it can be very difficult to remove the pellet again without firing it out, which is just what you don't want to do at the end of a long stalk!

11. Trajectory

Understanding your gun's trajectory is vital to successful shooting, and it is probably the area where most newcomers to the sport come unstuck. The principles are fairly simple, however, and you don't need a degree in physics to gain a good working knowledge of the subject.

An airgun pellet is subject to the same laws of motion as any other object. It will continue travelling in a straight line at the same speed unless some external force acts on it. It leaves the muzzle travelling at several hundred feet per second in a straight line. But as soon as it emerges into the open, two entirely separate forces start to act upon it. The first is gravity, which acts at 90 degrees to its line of flight – assuming you are shooting horizontally, which in most cases you will be. The external force of gravity will pull the pellet towards the earth. To begin with, the effect is hardly noticeable, because the pellet travels a long way in a very short space of time. The second force involved is air resistance – the force needed for the pellet to push its way through the air. This force also takes a while to have a noticeable effect, and for the first few yards the pellet will maintain its velocity with virtually no change. As the pellet travels through the air, however, the effect of both these forces begins to show. The pellet slows due to air resistance, and since it is travelling more slowly, the effect of gravity is more noticeable. The pellet starts to curve towards the earth more and more steeply, until eventually gravity takes over almost completely and the pellet is travelling at almost 90 degrees to its original direction, by which time it will probably have hit the ground.

It stands to reason that you must allow for this drop when you aim at the target. Light travels in straight lines, so the sights will draw a straight line to the target. You can adjust the sights so that they coincide with the pellet's flight path at a given distance, but at any other distance they will be either too high or too low. You must remember that the pellet starts its flight some way below the line of sight, since the sights are fixed above the barrel. In the case of open sights, this distance will be no more than half an inch, but for a scope on high mounts it could be as much as two inches. If you set the sights exactly parallel with the rifle's bore, the pellet would never meet the line of sight. It would start at, say, an inch below, and fall steadily further below it. The sights are always set so that the line of sight and the bore actually converge together. The pellet begins its flight below the line of sight, passes up through it, then slowly falls until it re-crosses the line and from that point onwards it falls further and further below it. A typical airgun will be zeroed at 25 yards or so. The pellet will pass through the line of sight at around 10 yards, rise above it for a few yards, reaching a peak at between 15 and 20 yards, then fall back through the line, crossing it again at 25 yards. In this example, you would have to aim high at a very close target at, say, 5 yards. At 10 yards you would aim dead on. Between 10 and 25 yards you would have to aim low, since the pellet is above the line of sight. At 25 yards you would aim dead on again, and beyond 25 yards you would need to aim high – increasing the 'holdover' as it is called, as the range lengthened.

ZEROING

An old tree stump provides a steady platform for a shot.

Knowing exactly where to aim for a target at a given range is one of the most difficult skills in airgun shooting. In theory it would be possible to calculate the necessary holdover or holdunder at any range, but in practice it is much easier to shoot a series of targets at different ranges, and map out the pellet's flight. You

start by zeroing the gun at your chosen range. To do this, you set up a paper target at the chosen range and, having first checked the background for safety, shoot a group of, say, five shots. Do not worry if the shots are off the bull. In fact it would be surprising if they were precisely on target. The important thing is to shoot a tight group. Then take the average of the five shots, and measure its distance from the aiming point – vertically and horizontally. Then adjust the sights to bring the pellets closer to the bull. Your sights may be marked with a scale showing you how much to turn them to move the point of impact a given distance at a certain range. Next, fire a second group, once again aiming at the bull. You may need to use a fresh target, or mark your first set of shots with a pen to avoid confusion. You should find that the second group is closer to the bull. Repeat the procedure until you can shoot a group that is centred exactly on the bullseye. Your rifle is now zeroed for that range – and that range only.

MAPPING OUT THE TRAJECTORY

Now you need to find out how the trajectory affects the aiming point at ranges closer and further away than your zero. To do this, set up a series of targets at measured ranges at, say, 5 yard intervals – starting with one at 5 yards and going as far as you like; 45 yards perhaps. Take your time, and shoot every shot as if it was the most important one. Stop for a break if you find yourself getting tired, because the results will be useless if you are not shooting normally.

At the end of this exercise, collect all the targets, clearly marking each one with its range when you pick it up. Then estimate the average point of impact on each target individually, and mark all the points on a graph, where the horizontal axis corresponds to the range, and the vertical axis shows the distance of the group above or below the aiming point. Join up all the points with a smooth curve, and you have a picture of your gun's trajectory. By reading off the distance on the horizontal axis, you can tell where the gun will shoot at any range you choose. I should point out that the results apply only to that particular combination of rifle and pellet. If you change to another type of pellet or replace your gun's mainspring, you will need to repeat the exercise from scratch.

Your series of targets will show you something else about your gun's performance – and your own. It will clearly illustrate how the size of the group increases with the range. At close ranges, you should be able to put all your pellets through the same hole, but as the range increases the group will become more spread out. It is this that effectively limits the range that you can shoot, far more than the loss of power as the pellet slows down. The pellet will still have sufficient power to kill a rabbit at 40 yards or more, but it is unlikely that you can be sure of hitting it in a vital spot at this range. It is highly irresponsible to shoot at a live animal when you cannot be sure of killing it cleanly, so you must exercise self restraint and only shoot at ranges where you know you can hit a vital spot. In practice, this means that the maximum group you should allow yourself is about 1½ inches across. If you can shoot a group that size at 40 yards then by all means shoot rabbits at that range. If, on the other hand, you can only be sure of putting all your pellets in a 1½ inch circle at 20 yards, then you should limit yourself to that range and no more.

ESTIMATING RANGE

Knowing the correct holdover or holdunder at any given range is all very well, but in the field you will not know the precise range of your target – and you can hardly expect a rabbit to sit still while you get the tape measure out! You must be able to estimate range reasonably accurately, certainly to the nearest 5 yards and preferably better. There is only one way to develop your skills of range estimation, and that is practice and plenty of it. Try to get into the habit of judging the range of each target before you take the shot. Don't think simply in terms of holdover; say to yourself, 'I think that is 27 yards away', not just 'I think that needs half an inch of holdover'.

And when you have taken the shot, regardless of whether you hit or miss, check the actual distance to see how accurate you were. You can even practise range estimation when you are walking along the street. Choose a point some distance away – a lamp-post, for example – which you are walking towards. Judge how far away you think it is, and then count the number of paces it takes you to reach it. It's more useful than not stepping on the cracks in the pavement, and you won't get so many strange looks either! You will need to work out the length of your stride so that you can convert your number of paces into an actual measurement. I am fortunate in that my steps measure almost exactly one yard, but yours may be longer or shorter. The way to do this is to pace out a good number of steps, say 50, using a stick or whatever comes to hand to mark your start and finish points. Use a tape measure to find out exactly how far it is between the two points, then divide the distance by the number of steps to find out the length of your average stride.

With a little practice you should find you can estimate range fairly accurately, although your first attempts are likely to be rather unreliable. In particular, you will find that the surroundings make a difference to your accuracy. It is much easier to judge the range when you have objects around to give your eyes a reference point, than for example a rabbit sitting in the middle of a bare field. Remember that rabbits vary in size, and what looks like a full-grown rabbit quite far away may be a younger one much closer. Once you can judge distances accurately, you can combine this skill with your knowledge of the rifle's trajectory to give you the precise amount of holdover required for each shot. It sounds simple enough, but if you can master these basic skills, you will be doing better than a great many airgunners.

RANGE FINDERS

I am not a great fan of measuring devices, although they can be useful in certain circumstances. They come in various forms: one type looks like a small camera through which you view the target. You will see a double image, and you turn a ring until the two images coincide to give a single picture of the target. You can then read off the range on a scale. Another type of rangefinder is built into a telescopic sight. This consists of a pair of horizontal lines on the reticule, a short distance apart. You look through the scope at the target, and adjust the scope's magnification with the zoom ring until the lines exactly bracket a known distance on the target. Typically, this might be the animal's head, or the distance between its shoulder and its chest. You can then read off the distance on the zoom ring, which is calibrated to show range as well as the power of magnification. I have only come across one example of this type of scope, and that is the Bisley scope from John Rothery Wholesale. From an airgunner's point of view, it suffers from the drawback that it is designed for big game hunting with a centrefire rifle, and the examples given in the instructions relate to quarry such as elk, mountain lion and coyote. You can still use the scope for airgun quarry at shorter ranges, but you will have to work out the conversion factors for yourself. You may find rangefinding devices like these helpful, but I don't believe they are a real substitute for developing your own skill in judging range. Once you have the knack, you will be able to estimate the range of your quarry with a glance, whereas a rangefinding device will always take a minute or two to operate.

WINDAGE

Just as you must allow for the effect that gravity has in dragging the pellet downwards, you must also take account of the wind blowing the pellet to the side. In a stiff breeze, the pellet may be deflected by an inch or two on its way to the target, which is enough to make the difference between a hit or a miss. Allowing for wind is very difficult, and the best advice is to stay at home if there is more than a light breeze. There will be occasions when this is not possible, perhaps when you are competing in a field target shoot, and you will have to cope as best you can. If the wind is steady, you may decide to re-zero your rifle to allow for it, but usually the wind will vary from one minute to the next. If this is the case, time your shot so that you fire when the wind drops. If a gust comes along as you are lining up on the target, wait for it to subside. Not only will the wind affect the pellet, but it will also make it much more difficult to hold the rifle steady. The difficult part is knowing how much to aim off for a given strength of wind at a given distance. This is something that you can only really find out by trial and error, because it will depend on your rifle and pellet combination. If you think you may have to shoot in the wind, make sure you get in as much practice as possible beforehand.

SHOOTING UPHILL

Before we leave the subject of trajectory and range, let me say a few words about shooting up or down hill – something which often causes problems. We saw earlier how gravity begins to act upon a pellet the moment it leaves the muzzle. When you are shooting parallel to the ground, the force of gravity is at 90 degrees to the pellet's line of flight. Imagine now that you are shooting directly up at the sky. Gravity is acting back along the pellet's path, in the same direction as the air resistance. The pellet will therefore slow down more quickly, but there is no force at 90 degrees to the line of flight. It will follow a straight line, rather than the curved trajectory that we saw before. Since the barrel and the line of sight are aligned on a converging angle, the pellet will pass through the line of sight at roughly the same point as before – about 10 yards from the muzzle. But it will then continue to rise above the line of sight, instead of reaching a peak and falling back through it. So for any range beyond 10 yards, you will have to aim further and further below the point where you want the pellet to strike. The same principle applies if you are shooting directly downwards towards the centre of the earth, although it is difficult to imagine a situation in which this would apply. Shooting a rat at the bottom of a well, perhaps! The difference is that the pellet will tend to speed up under the influence of gravity, rather than slowing down – but there is still no force acting at 90 degrees to the pellet's path to produce the familiar curved trajectory.

Now, it is very unlikely that you will be shooting straight up or down. More probably, you may be aiming at 45 degrees, perhaps at a pigeon in a tree. In this case, the effect of gravity is mid-way between two extremes, and the pellet will follow a trajectory which is mid-way between these two examples. Suppose that your rifle is zeroed at 25 yards, so that if you were shooting horizontally, you would aim straight at a target at that range. Let us also suppose that if you were shooting vertically, you would need to aim three inches under the target at that range. Well, for a target 25 yards away at 45 degrees, you would aim mid-way between the two – that is, 1½ inches below the target.

The same principle applies to the allowance you must make for the wind. If the wind is straight towards you, or following the path of the pellet, you can ignore it. If it is blowing at 45 degrees to the direction of the shot, you must allow half the amount for drift that you would if it was blowing at 90 degrees.

In the next chapter, we will look at the various types of airgun sights, and see how some types of scope actually allow you to dial in the amount of holdover or windage that you need, so you can aim dead-on – which can be more accurate than deliberately aiming off by a certain amount.

12. Airgun sights

You might think that the subject of sights should have come into Chapter 2, which covered the different parts of the airgun and how they work. But the sights are such an important part of the gun that they really need a chapter to themselves and it also helps if you have read about trajectories first.

Airgun sights fall into two main categories. First, there are the open type, which you find on most airguns when they come out of the box. They consist of two parts: the foresight on the muzzle end of the barrel, and a rearsight nearer your eye. The second type is the optical sight, normally a telescopic sight, or scope for short, which you fit onto the scope rails on the gun's cylinder.

OPEN SIGHTS

Let's look at open sights first. Most serious airgunners buy a scope as soon as possible, and don't use open sights if they can help it. Scopes certainly have their advantages, but don't assume that open sights are no good. They can be extremely accurate at normal ranges, and they have the added advantage that there is very little to go wrong. Once or twice in my shooting career, I have had a scope fail in the field, and I have been very glad to be able to use the open sights as a back-up.

A typical set of open sights will consist of a blade foresight and a notch rearsight. When you hold the gun up to your shoulder, the rearsight will appear as a black silhouette with a notch cut in the top edge. The foresight is a narrow post which you line up in the centre of the notch. Some foresights have a tunnel-shaped protector over the top, to stop them being knocked and damaged. This can help you to line up the sights more quickly, because it appears as a circle with the foresight in the centre.

To aim, you line up the foresight in the rearsight notch, and at the same time hold the foresight on the target. That sounds simple enough, but of course there is more to it than that. First of all, the foresight and rearsight must be lined up correctly. The top of the foresight should be level with the top of the rearsight notch. It must also be perfectly centred between the sides of the notch, with exactly the same amount of 'air' on either side. Some people like to blot out the aiming mark with the foresight blade, but I find it more accurate to sit the aiming mark just above the tip of the blade. Even so, there will be occasions when you have to allow holdover, and find you have to blot out the target. Whichever system you prefer, you must stick to it, because changing from one to the other will alter the point of impact.

Like any sighting system, open sights must be zeroed to suit the gun's trajectory at a predetermined range. You do this in the same way as with any other type of sight, by setting up a paper target at your chosen range, firing a group of shots, and altering the sights to bring the group to your aiming point. Most open sights are adjusted by screws on the rearsight, which move the notch up, down, left and right. Moving the rearsight in a given direction will move the point of impact in the same direction. If your group hits the target too high and to the right, for instance, you would move the rearsight down and to the left. Most foresights are fixed firmly to the barrel, and cannot be adjusted, but a few are adjustable in a limited way – usually by removing the fixing screw to move them up or down. This is a crude adjustment so that you can bring the sights roughly into line before making the final adjustments with the rearsight. If you do this, remember that you must move the foresight in the opposite direction to the rearsight – up to bring the point of impact down, and vice versa.

One of the biggest problems with open sights is that it is impossible to focus your eye on the rearsight, foresight and target all at once. You must develop the knack of looking from one to the other quickly, without moving your eye, so you can judge when all three are lined up correctly. Some people, especially older shooters, find this very difficult. The aperture type of rearsight used by target shooters gets round this problem to some extent, because the tiny aperture helps to focus the foresight and target more clearly, and there is no need to bring the rearsight into sharp focus. Aperture sights are very difficult to use in the field, however, because they are designed for shooting at simple circular targets. If you aim one at a rabbit, for instance, it can be very difficult to make out the target clearly, and judging holdover is virtually impossible because of the restricted field of view.

The other drawback of open sights for field shooting, whether at competition targets or live quarry, is that they are much less accurate in poor light. This is largely due to the limitations of the human eye, which does not make out detail so accurately in semi-darkness. The open sights do not stand out well against a dark background, so shooting at dawn and dusk is severely restricted. You can improve things slightly by putting a dab of paint on the foresight blade – red nail varnish works quite well, in fact. This will give you an extra 10 or 15 minutes' shooting at dusk, but for serious shooting in poor light there is no substitute for a good optical sight.

TELESCOPIC SIGHTS

A scope works on an entirely different principle from open sights. You look through it rather than at it, just as you would look through a telescope or a pair of binoculars. The lenses in the scope are arranged so as to project an image of the target onto your eye, and a set of cross-hairs built into the scope appear superimposed on the image. The cross-hairs are focused in the same plane as the image, so you don't have to alter the focus of your eye to see when they are on target.

The other great advantage of a scope over open sights is that it magnifies the image, so you see the target more clearly than you could with the naked eye. This allows you to shoot more accurately, and in poorer light, than you could with open sights. As with open sights, you must zero the scope for the trajectory of your gun/pellet combination at your chosen range, and you do this by means of the windage and elevation screws which are under the protective caps in the centre of the scope tube. These screws move the cross-hairs in relation to the image, allowing you to adjust the point of impact until it coincides with your aiming mark. The elevation and windage adjustment screws on some scopes are raised well above the scope tube, with calibrations on them so you can make your adjustments without having to remove the caps. The idea is that you can adjust the zero of the scope for each shot, so you do not have to allow any holdover or holdunder. You must know how many clicks to turn the screws for a given distance, of course, and this requires plenty of practice. You first zero the scope in the normal way, then remove the calibrated cap, taking care not to twist the screw off the setting you have found. Then replace the cap so that the 'O' is lined up with the mark on the scope tube, so you can always return to your zero setting when you want. You must then practise at different ranges, until you have found how many clicks to turn the adjuster for each range.

Parts of the scope

The end of the scope nearest to your eye when you shoot is called the ocular end, and the lens in the bell there is known as the ocular lens. The ocular bell will twist so you can focus the scope to suit your eyesight and the ranges you will be shooting at. Once you have decided on the best setting, you can lock it in place by tightening up the locking ring. Many scopes have a rubber ring around the end of the ocular bell to protect your face if you should knock it. This is unlikely to happen on an airgun, but a lot of scopes were originally designed for powerful cartridge rifles which have a hefty recoil.

The ocular bell and zoom adjustment ring of a Tasco scope.

At the furthest end of the scope, known as the object end, you will find the object lens. This lens has an important effect on the scope's performance, and it is this lens which is referred to in the scope's specification. A specification consists of two figures, such as 4 × 20, or 3–9 × 40. The first figure or figures refer to the scope's magnification, that is to say the degree to which it magnifies the image of what you are looking at. A 4× scope, for instance, will magnify the image four times, so your target will look four times closer than it actually is. Some scopes, called zoom scopes, allow you to alter the magnification by turning a ring at the ocular end of the tube. The second figure in the scope's specification gives the size of the object lens in millimetres – so a 4 × 40 scope will have an object lens which measures 40mm in diameter.

The object lens is important because it is the one that determines the amount of light which can enter the lens. Clearly, a bigger lens will let more light into the scope. A series of lenses inside the scope then focus this circle of light down and into your eye. The degree to which this circle is reduced in size determines the magnification. If the circle is reduced from 40mm to 10mm then the magnification is 4 ×.

You might think that you could go on increasing the size of the object lens to let in more and more light, allowing you to shoot in virtual darkness. This isn't the case, however. As with open sights, the human eye is the limiting factor. As we have seen, a bigger object lens means a bigger circle of light being projected from the ocular end of the scope. This circle of light is called the exit pupil, and up to a point the bigger it is, the better you will see in poor light. But the human eye imposes its own limitations once again. The pupil in your eye can enlarge to let in more light in dim conditions, but for most people the maximum size of the pupil is 7mm, even in pitch darkness. The eye can only make use of light which actually falls through the pupil. Any light outside that area is wasted. So enlarging the exit pupil of the scope beyond 7mm does not help.

To calculate the exit pupil size you divide the object lens size by the magnification. For a typical airgun scope with a magnification of 4 × and a 32mm object lens, the exit pupil measures 8mm. A bigger object lens, such as a 40mm, increases the amount of light passing through the scope, but the extra light falls outside the pupil of your eye and doesn't help you to see any better. Where a bigger object lens can be an advantage is

The parallax adjustment ring on the objective bell of a telescopic sight.

in allowing you to use a higher magnification. With a 56mm object lens, for instance, you could use a magnification of 8 × and still have an exit pupil of 7mm. Mind you, I am not very keen on high magnification, because it simply magnifies any wobble and I don't believe it helps you to shoot more accurately. What it can do is give you the false impression that you can be more accurate, encouraging you to take risky long shots.

Some scopes these days have another adjustment in addition to the windage, elevation, focus and zoom. This is called parallax adjustment, and it consists of a ring on the object bell marked in distances from about 10 yards to infinity. Parallax is a problem that all scopes suffer from to a certain extent. It stems from the fact that the reticule is fixed at a set point in the scope tube, while the lenses focus the image differently according to the range. If the image is not focused precisely on the reticule, then when you move your eye in relation to the scope, the cross-hairs will appear to move across the target, even though you are holding the gun completely still. The result is that you may be aiming at a different point from where you think, if you bring the gun up slightly differently from one shot to the next – and no one can repeat precisely the same position every time. This error – called parallax error – can cause you to miss the target by an inch or more, and it is a particular problem when you are using a scope designed for centrefire rifle shooting at airgun ranges.

The parallax adjustment allows you to 'dial out' parallax error by setting the ring to the distance of your target. This has the effect of focusing the image exactly on the reticule, thereby eliminating parallax error. I find that it also helps to bring the target and reticule into exactly the same focus, making aiming easier.

Choosing a scope

So much for the various parts of the scope, but how do you go about choosing which one is best for your needs? The first step is to decide on your budget, because you can spend anything from £10 to £150 and upwards. As a general rule, the more expensive the better, although extra features obviously add to the cost of the scope, and they may not improve your performance. My advice would be to go for a simple scope without a lot of gimmicks. That way you get better quality for your money. As for the specification, I reckon you can't beat 4 × 32 as a good, all-round airgun scope. It has plenty of magnification for normal airgun ranges, and the object lens is big enough to transmit all the light your eye can use. Parallax adjustment is a useful feature, to my mind, and I think it represents money well spent.

I am not particularly keen on zoom scopes, although some people swear by them. I find that I set the zoom on 4 ×, and then don't alter it from one year to the next, so what is the point of paying extra? It is possible to use a zoom as an aid to judging the range of your target, and in this case the extra cost could well be justified. The Bisley rangefinder scope distributed by John Rothery has a special double horizontal cross-hair to help with estimating range, and the zoom ring is marked with ranges in yards. You zoom the scope in or out until the twin cross-hairs bracket a given measurement on your quarry, then read off the range from the ring. Unfortunately, the scope is calibrated for big game shooting, so the scale reads in hundreds of yards for quarry such as elk and coyote. It is possible to convert the results into normal airgun ranges, provided you spend a little time working out the figures first, and select a known measurement on your typical quarry – the height of a rabbit's head, for instance. A nice touch on this particular scope is that the elevation adjustment is the turret or silhouette type, and it is

The Bisley 'Range-finder' scope has ranges marked on the zoom ring.

calibrated to correspond with the ranges on the zoom ring. In theory, you would read off the distance from the zoom ring, and then dial that range into the elevation screw or 'bullet drop compensator'. This would allow for the bullet's trajectory,

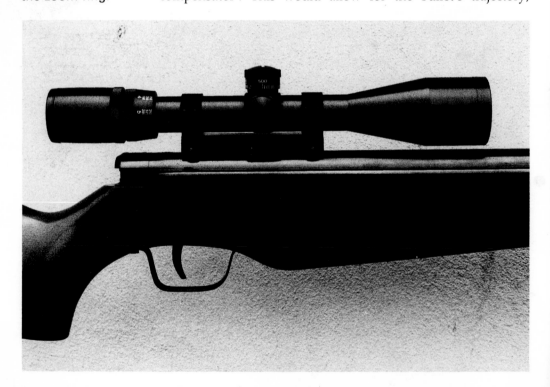

making it possible to aim dead-on at any range. Once again, you would have to spend some time working out how to convert the figures for airgun shooting, but it could well be worth the effort.

In fact, you can do the same thing with an ordinary zoom scope, provided it has a duplex or 30–30 reticule. This is the most common type of reticule, which consists of four thick posts in a cross shape, with very fine cross-hairs in the centre. This reticule is popular because it lets you bring the gun onto the target quickly by looking at the thick posts, while the fine cross-hairs allow very accurate aiming. To use it for rangefinding, you would bracket a known measurement (such as a rabbit's head) between the centre cross and the end of one of the thick posts, zooming in or out until the two matched exactly. You would then multiply the reading on the zoom scale by 'factor X' to find

A range of scopes from one manufacturer – in this case Optima – illustrates the many different specifications available. These range from a 4 × 32 to a 3–9 × 56 with parallax adjustment.

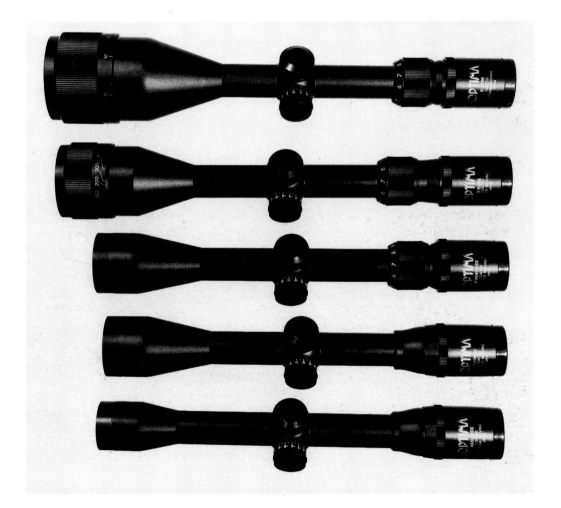

the range. Factor X depends on the measurement you have chosen to bracket, and can only be found by trial and error.

Having decided on the specification of the scope, your next decision must be based on its quality. This is difficult to judge, although the price and the manufacturer's reputation will be a good guide. One test which can be useful is to hold the scope up to your eye, and turn slowly round, looking all the time for unwelcome reflections or highlights which spoil the image. On a poor quality scope, you will find that light is reflected from the surface of the lenses, and causes distracting flashes of light. Better quality scopes have a coating of magnesium fluoride on the lenses to cut down these reflections and improve the image.

Another way to assess the quality is to remove the windage and elevation adjustment caps, and turn the screws a few clicks to see how they feel. On a good scope, they will turn easily but positively, with a clearly defined click from one position to the next.

The most important thing of all about any scope is the quality

A range of scopes from the British gunmakers BSA, including a 4 × 20 (foreground), and a parallax adjustable zoom model (fitted to the rifle).

Silhouette type windage and eleva-tion turrets.

of the image, and the only way to assess this is to look through it, preferably in comparison with other scopes to give you a benchmark. Points to look for are the brightness of the image, and its sharpness – not just in the centre around the cross-hairs, but also on the outer edges of the image. Most lenses will give you a good crisp image in the centre of the picture, but only the better ones can keep the image pin-sharp at the edges, especially on high magnification. Similarly, the image from a poor scope may become darker around the edges. The toughest test for any scope is to look through it in poor light, as night is falling. Once again, it is best to have at least two scopes side by side so you can compare one with the other. Use a target such as a newspaper, and check which scope allows you to read the print the longest as night draws in.

It is a good idea to visit a gunshop and look at the range of scopes available in your price range because this will allow you to compare one scope with another. Don't be afraid to ask the gunsmith's advice about your choice of scope. He will be able to tell you if a particular scope is reliable, for instance, because he will know whether he has had any returned because they have broken in use. One of the most fragile components of a scope is the reticule, which normally consists of a very fine piece of metal foil cut to the correct shape. This foil can easily be broken if you drop the scope, or if you try to take it apart. One scope distributed by Gunmark has the reticule etched onto one of the lenses inside, however, which means that you cannot break the reticule unless you break the lens, which is much more robust than a thin piece of foil. In fact, the manufacturers say that well over half the scopes returned for repair are suffering from broken reticules, so anything that makes this less likely could be a good idea.

Most scopes are finished in black, either polished or matt. The matt finish is normally preferable for hunting, since it is less likely to catch the light and alarm your quarry. Some scopes have a coating of rubber 'armour' which protects them from the inevitable knocks and scratches in the field. The rubber is usually black, but it also comes in a camouflage pattern of greens and browns, which can be useful for hunting.

SCOPE MOUNTS

A large scope such as this 56mm requires high mounts to fit it to the gun.

When you set out to buy a scope, remember to leave yourself enough money in the kitty to buy a good set of mounts. The mounts are vitally important, because even the best scope is worse than useless if it is not mounted to the gun firmly so it cannot move when you fire. Scope 'creep' is a problem which many airgunners have come up against. It describes the

movement of the scope and its mounts along the scope rail, under the recoil of the gun when it is fired. The scope may only move a fraction of an inch with each shot, but over a number of shots it will move far enough to make a big difference to the scope's alignment. Strange as it may seem, scope creep can be more of a problem on an airgun than on a powerful cartridge rifle. This is because of the relatively harsh recoil of a spring air rifle. The simplest way to overcome scope creep is to fit an arrestor block, which is a block of metal that fits onto the scope rails behind the mounts, and prevents them moving backwards along the rail. Nowadays, however, you can buy some excellent one-piece mounts which have a much larger area of metal in contact with the scope rails than the traditional two-piece mounts, and provided you fit them correctly will not creep. You should be careful not to over-tighten the screws on the scope mounts, incidentally, because you could damage the scope, the rails or the mount itself.

ILLUMINATED AIMING MARKS

An illuminated red dot sight. The cap on top of the ocular bell houses a small battery which powers the aiming dot.

One of the characteristics of airgunners is that they are constantly trying to improve their equipment, and this applies just as much to sights as anything else. Shooting in poor light is one area where man's ingenuity has been applied to developing better systems to make the job just that little bit easier. There have been various attempts to make scopes with illuminated aiming marks which will allow the shooter to aim accurately despite poor light. Most of these have been based on an illuminated red dot at the centre of the cross-hairs. This is

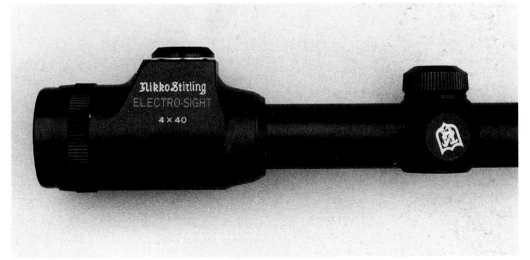

usually powered by a small battery contained in a housing on the scope tube, with a switch to turn the tiny bulb inside on and off. These can be very effective, because it is normally the cross-hairs which disappear first as the light fails. You can see the target, but the cross-hairs melt into the dark background and you cannot be sure of your aiming mark. With an illuminated red dot, the mark stands out like a beacon, and the limiting factor becomes being able to see the target rather than the cross-hairs. One manufacturer has now gone one step further, by bringing out a scope which will allow you to illuminate the entire reticule, not just the centre point. Not only that, but you can also alter the colour of the reticule by turning a ring, so you can choose a colour which contrasts well against any background.

ADVANCED SIGHTING SYSTEMS

The Focal Point sight, a red dot type of aiming device, fitted to a Saxby and Palmer air cartridge rifle.

Many other sighting systems have been tried besides open sights and scopes, and a good few of these have their origins in military research and development. The Singlepoint red dot sight, for instance, was neither an open sight nor a scope. It worked by producing a narrow beam of red light which was projected back into the shooter's aiming eye. The aiming eye saw a red dot, surrounded by a black circle. By keeping the other eye open, you appeared to see the target with the red dot aiming mark superimposed on it. This sight did not magnify the

target, of course, but it did allow you to bring the gun to the aim very quickly. Many airgunners found that the red dot was too large for accurate shooting at normal airgun ranges, however. At 20 yards or so, it would completely obliterate a rabbit's head, while a scope, being much more precise, would allow you to aim at a specific point on the quarry's head.

Military night sights of the image intensifier type have always held an attraction for airgunners, but their high cost has prevented them being used by all but the wealthiest enthusiasts. Another sight which falls into the same category is the laser sight, which projects a small red dot onto the target itself. You simply place the dot on the point you wish to hit, and fire. Having tried one of these, I was disappointed to find that the laser spot is very dim – so dim, in fact, that it is only of any use when shooting at night.

Attractive as these sights may sound, they are unlikely to take over from the scope as the airgunner's favourite sighting system. Indeed, there is currently a trend towards the simpler types of sight, with the most popular being the basic 4 × 32 with no extras such as parallax adjustment or bullet drop compensation. I suspect the scope, like the spring airgun, will be with us for many years to come.

13.   Airgun equipment

Fishermen are often accused of being obsessed with the ancillary equipment that goes with their sport, and it is certainly true that some of them collect far more flies, floats and so on than they could ever use in a lifetime of fishing. I sometimes wonder whether airgunners aren't guilty of the same obsession. When I look at my shelves full of knives, pellet holders, gun covers and goodness knows what, I have to admit that only a fraction of it all is really necessary. The trouble is that it's so much fun collecting odds and ends that just might come in useful one day.

Let's look at some of the more popular items, and how they can help, either by improving your performance, or simply making shooting easier and more comfortable.

TARGET HOLDERS

Perhaps one of the first bits of equipment that many shooters consider buying is a target holder of some sort. You can make do with empty shotgun shells, old drinks cans, and the sides of cardboard boxes, but for zeroing your gun or practising your marksmanship, there is really nothing to beat a proper paper target. Anything that you pin a target to is likely to be battered to pieces in a fairly short time by the hail of lead pellets hitting it, so a purpose-built target holder is very useful. It will allow you to change targets quickly by simply slipping the old one out and a new one in, and it will halt the pellet in mid-flight so that it cannot do any damage. The simplest form of target holder is a sheet of metal bent to provide grooves either side into which the target card fits. This is the type that BSA include in the box with their airguns, and it does a perfectly good job. You can buy more elaborate holders which are designed to trap the pellet. These have an angled back plate which directs the pellet downwards and into a collection area, where the deformed spent pellets collect until you decide to empty it. This type is excellent if you have some use for the scrap lead – perhaps because you are planning to cast your own pellets. Whichever type of target holder you decide upon, it is a good idea to choose the targets you intend to use first, and then buy a holder to fit. Paper targets come in all shapes and sizes, and you don't want to restrict yourself to using a target that you do not like simply because it is the only one that will fit your holder.

PELLET HOLDERS

Looking at my shelves, the next piece of equipment is a pellet holder. This is designed to hold a number of pellets where they are protected from damage, but easily accessible for rapid reloading in the field. There are many different types, some for fitting onto the gun itself, and others that you wear on your body, often strapped round your arm or on your belt. Most of them consist of a block of soft rubbery material with a number of holes into which you insert the pellets. The rubber is stiff enough to hold the pellets in place, but will not mark or damage them. This is a great improvement on the more common methods of carrying pellets – either in their original tin or loose in a pocket. A tin will rattle and alarm the quarry, while pellets in a pocket can easily be damaged, and will leave lead inside which can be transferred via your hands to food and threaten your health. I once knew a keen airgunner who carried spare pellets in his mouth when he was out hunting, which seems to be asking for a case of lead poisoning.

PELLET SIZERS AND DISPENSERS

I have already mentioned pellet sizers in the chapter on ammunition. These gadgets allow you to make tiny adjustments to the diameter of the pellet's skirt, and so ensure that every pellet is exactly the same size. This removes the tiny variations in diameter which you inevitably find in any batches of pellets, and in theory at least means that your gun will shoot more accurately. A pellet sizer can also help if you are using British pellets in a foreign gun. The British .22 calibre measures 5.6mm in diameter, whereas European guns are designed to take 5.5mm ammunition. That 0.1mm can make it very difficult to fit a British pellet into the breech of a foreign gun, and a pellet sizer will allow you to bring it down to the right size for an easy fit.

Certain types of pellet require a special dispenser so you can seat them properly into the breech. The Sabo is a case in point. This is a two-piece pellet which you make up by fitting the metal 'bullet' into the plastic sabot. The pellet must then be placed in the breech, and if you try to do this with your fingers the sabot will spring open and the bullet will drop out. You need to use the special dispenser which is supplied with the pellets. This consists of a plastic tube into which you place the sabot before pushing the bullet into position. You can then hold the end of the tube against the breech, and use the plunger to push the pellet into position.

You can also buy pellet dispensers for ordinary pellets, which are designed for rapid reloading. The dispenser holds several pellets at once, keeping them safe from damage. You cock the gun in the usual way, then push a pellet into the breech using the dispenser. This is particularly useful when you are shooting in difficult conditions, because it saves fumbling for your pellets with cold, gloved hands.

GUN SLEEVES AND COVERS

A gun sleeve is an indispensable piece of equipment, in my opinion. The law stipulates that an airgun must be carried in a securely fastened cover in certain circumstances, so without one you are seriously restricted in where you can legally take your gun. A cover also serves to protect it against damp, dirt and damage when you are not actually shooting, and it is good practice to get into the habit of putting the gun in its sleeve as soon as you have finished for the journey home. Do remember that any damp and dirt on the gun will be transferred to the lining of the sleeve, and in the confined space can quickly cause rust. For this reason I prefer the type which has a zip running down the length of the sleeve, so you can open it right out to allow it to dry and clean off any dirt. Gun sleeves come in many different shapes and sizes, ranging from the very cheap ones made of a single layer of material, to expensive sheepskin lined versions. The cheapest type offer little protection against knocks, but they are better than nothing. It is better, though, to go for a slightly more expensive model which will provide some padding and cushion the gun from damage if something should fall on it in the boot of the car, for instance.

SLINGS

Many people think of a sling as a means of carrying a gun over your shoulder. Certainly it will do that, but the main purpose of a sling is to help you to aim more accurately by steadying your hold. To use a sling, hold the gun around the pistol grip with your right hand (assuming you are right-handed). Pass your left arm through the loop of the sling from left to right, then bring your left hand round under the sling from right to left, so that the sling wraps round your arm. Now grasp the fore-end in the usual way, and bring the stock into your right shoulder. The sling should now be taut – if it isn't, then it needs to be adjusted to the right length. The tension in the sling will hold the gun firmly in your shoulder, giving you a much steadier hold than you could achieve otherwise.

Few airguns come fitted with sling swivels, so you will have to take your weapon to a gunsmith if you want to use a sling. The normal positions for the swivels are one on the underside of the stock near the toe, and one one-third of the way down the barrel. This is not possible with some airguns, particularly the break-barrel type, because the tension on the sling will tend to pull the barrel open. The gunsmith will be able to advise you where the forward swivel should be fitted. Sometimes you can successfully fit it on the barrel just ahead of the hinge pin; on other guns it may be better on the breech block. Once you have the swivels in place, the choice of sling is up to you. There are many different types, but they all do the same job. You can even have one with your name woven into the material, or punched into the surface of a leather sling. The width of the sling is important, because it must be broad enough that it won't cut into your arm uncomfortably when you shoot. If it is too broad, however, it can prevent you bending your elbow easily, especially if it is the stiff leather type. The ideal width, to my mind, is 1½ inches. It is important to choose a sling that you can adjust easily for length, because if it is too long or too short, then it will hinder rather than help your shooting.

SILENCERS

One of the most popular pieces of kit for hunting is a silencer, which fits on the muzzle and cuts down the noise of the escaping air when you fire. It is misleading to call these devices silencers, in fact, because they do not really make the gun silent. 'Sound moderators' would be more accurate, although everyone uses the name silencer. An airgun silencer works in the same way as the silencer on a car. It consists of an outer tube which forms an expansion chamber to allow the air to exit the barrel in a more controlled way. A series of baffles inside the tube increase the effect. These are discs with a hole in the centre to allow the pellet to pass freely through, while holding up the rush of air behind it. A silencer is most effective on a pneumatic airgun, because the mechanical noise made by these guns is tiny – no more than a slight click as the hammer hits the valve stem. With a spring airgun, much of the noise comes from the spring and piston, which is unaffected by the silencer. I once carried out a test which suggested that the effect of a silencer is most noticeable to the side of the gun, while the noise coming out directly towards the target was not greatly affected. This seems to be supported by my experience, which is that with a silencer

The standard mounts on this pistol and rifle will accept any of the four silencers shown.

you are less likely to alarm wildlife on either side, while any creature roughly in the line of fire will still take fright, due to a combination of the noise of the gun's discharge and the sound of the pellet whizzing through the air. Even so, quarry will sometimes be confused by the sound, and will freeze in its tracks rather than making for cover.

OTHER EQUIPMENT

There are many other gadgets used by airgunners, both home-made like the foam seats carried by field target competitors, and specially designed such as decoys and calls for hunting. These and others will be covered in later chapters in the appropriate sections, but try to remember the guiding principle: by all means buy these bits and pieces if you enjoy collecting them, but leave them at home unless they are going to be really useful – otherwise you'll look like a Christmas tree, and wear yourself out carrying all that clobber!

14. The law

In Britain, we are fortunate to be given a great deal of freedom in what we do without interference from the authorities. There are various laws that apply to shooting with an airgun, however. These are designed to protect the public against irresponsible use of airguns, and to protect certain species of birds and animals. By and large, the laws are plain common sense, and if you use your gun responsibly you are unlikely to find yourself on the wrong side of the law. You need to know exactly what you are and are not allowed to do, because ignorance is no defence if you break the law, and the penalties are severe.

Please bear in mind that the following guidelines are only my interpretation of the law, which is actually phrased in the usual legal jargon. The law can be changed at any time, too, so you should make sure that you are fully up to date. The British Association for Shooting and Conservation publishes leaflets explaining the law relating to shooting in more detail, and will also advise members on specific points. For that reason alone, you would be well advised to join if you are not already a member, although I would strongly advise you to join the BASC anyway because of all the good work they do to represent shooters and look after their interests.

THE LEGAL POWER LIMIT

In mainland Britain, you can own an air rifle with a muzzle energy up to 12 ft lbs, or an air pistol up to 6 ft lbs, without any form of certificate, provided you are over seventeen. If the gun is more powerful than this you will need to obtain a firearms certificate, for which you must apply to your local police. A firearms certificate is also required if you live in Northern Ireland. The restrictions on firearms certificate weapons are much stricter, and the police will probably want to visit your home to interview you about where the gun will be kept and used before the certificate is granted. The police also have the right to refuse to grant you a certificate if they choose.

An airgun's muzzle energy may vary with different pellets, so it is a good idea to chronograph your gun with your chosen pellets to check that it does not exceeed the legal limit. If it does, you should take it to a gunsmith immediately and have it 'detuned' so that it is legal once again. You might be tempted to try to increase your gun's power so that it is above the legal limit. Don't. Not only are you risking prosecution, but you are unlikely to be making your gun any more effective. Remember that accuracy is more important than power. If you can place your pellet where you want it, then 10 ft lbs is more than enough to do the job. The legal limit of 12 ft lbs for an air rifle means that a .22 pellet can leave the muzzle at over 600 feet per second, and a .177 pellet at nearly 800 fps, which is perfectly adequate for normal shooting at live quarry or field targets. Concentrate on improving your accuracy, not your gun's power.

AIRGUNS IN PUBLIC PLACES

So much for the gun, but where can you use it? The simple answer is, only on land that you actually own, or where you have the specific permission of the landowner. You are not allowed to shoot on roads or footpaths, on common land, parks, or any land where you do not have the landowner's permission. If you do, you run the risk of being prosecuted for armed trespass – a very serious offence. You must also make sure that your pellets do not stray outside the boundaries of the land where you are allowed to shoot, so that rules out shooting at anything above ground level in your back garden, for instance. You are not allowed to shoot within 50 feet of a public road or footpath where doing so is 'likely to cause a nuisance' – which might mean that someone walking along the path is alarmed by a sudden shot close by. This rule applies even to land owned by yourself, so if your garden is very close to the road, you must be especially careful. Even if you are not near a road, it makes sense to spare a thought for your neighbours. There have been many clay pigeon shooting grounds which have been forced to close because people living nearby have complained that they cause a nuisance, and in theory there is no reason why the same thing shouldn't happen to airgunners.

WHERE YOU CAN SHOOT

The law states that an airgun must be unloaded if you are carrying it in a public place – which means anywhere that the general public have a right to be. The term 'unloaded' is a difficult one in the case of an airgun. You might think that it was unloaded if you uncocked it by releasing the mainspring, but having a pellet in the breech could still count as being loaded. To be on the safe side, remove the pellet and uncock the gun and that way there cannot be any argument. An air pistol must not only be unloaded, but also in a securely fastened case when you are in a public place. There are special restrictions on younger people carrying airguns in public places. If you are under seventeen, even an air rifle must be unloaded and inside a securely fastened case. In fact, the sight of a gun is likely to alarm people who do not know about guns, so it is a good idea to keep any gun in a case in public, regardless of your age.

YOUNGER SHOOTERS

Between the ages of fourteen and seventeen, you can borrow an airgun and ammunition, or be given it as a present, but you cannot go out and buy it for yourself, or hire it. The person giving or lending you the gun or ammo must be over seventeen themselves, of course. If you are under fourteen years old, you cannot be given or lent an airgun or ammunition, even as a present. And you can only use an airgun while you are under the direct supervision of someone over twenty-one years old. This applies even in your own back garden, and the person supervising you must be with you all the time you are shooting, and must not leave you alone with the gun even for a minute.

WHAT YOU CAN SHOOT

There are laws protecting wildlife which apply whatever type of gun you are using. Everyone knows that some animals and birds are protected, and these include many of the common garden birds such as blackbirds and robins as well as rarities like ospreys. There are some species of animal which, although you may shoot them with more powerful cartridge rifles, are too large for a clean kill with an airgun. These include all the deer, and foxes. The law stipulates the size of bullet that you can use for deer shooting, and a normal airgun pellet would be far too small. I am not aware of any such restriction on foxes, but I hope that no airgunner would attempt to kill a fox with an airgun. You would be far too likely to injure it – and there are other laws which make it an offence to cause unnecessary suffering to any creature, regardless of whether it is a protected species or not. All this brings the list of legitimate airgun quarry down to a relatively few species, most notably: crows, rooks, woodpigeons, collared doves, feral pigeons, magpies, jays, brown rats, grey squirrels and rabbits. Make sure you can recognise the quarry species, and if you are in any doubt, don't shoot. Remember that just because the law allows you to shoot a certain species, it doesn't mean that you should try to exterminate it with no regard for the balance of nature in your area. There are places where magpies are a serious pest and need to be controlled, for instance, but before you shoot a magpie in your back garden, ask yourself if it is really doing anyone any harm. Do not take life just for the sake of it, or you are no better than the vermin you are pretending to control.

That covers the main rules regulating what you can shoot and where, but there are other laws of the land which you will come across when you follow the sport of airgunning. Sooner or later, you may buy a gun or piece of equipment which you feel does not live up to your expectations, or the promises made in the advertising. This can be a problem when you buy equipment by mail order, through an advertisement in a magazine, for instance.

CONSUMER PROTECTION

There are laws intended to protect the consumer – you and me – against unscrupulous traders who sell shoddy goods or make false claims. Consumer protection law is a complicated subject, with various Consumer Protection and Trade Descriptions Acts, and it can be difficult to understand exactly what your rights are.

Basically, when you buy something from a trader, you are entitled to assume that it is fit for the purpose for which it was sold. In other words, if you buy an airgun, you can expect it to fire pellets with reasonable accuracy and power, bearing in mind its price. If it breaks after the first half dozen shots due to some fault in its manufacture, you are entitled to your money back, or a replacement. However, if you drop it on the ground and break it, that's not the gunshop's fault, and you will have to pay to have it repaired. Similarly, the gun, scope or whatever should live up to the claims made in the advertising. If the advertisement said an air rifle was 'bang on the legal limit', and it could only manage 5 ft lbs, then you would be entitled to ask for your money back. The law allows for an element of poetic licence or 'puffery' in advertising, so you might not have a case if you didn't agree that such-and-such a gun was 'the best thing since sliced bread', but technical specifications in advertising must be accurate. I should point out that you don't have the same protection from the law if you buy from a private individual rather than a dealer.

So what do you do if your brand new gun breaks down, or your scope falls in half when you turn the zoom ring? The first thing is to check the warranty. Most manufacturers give some kind of warranty, which gives you extra rights over and above the rights granted to you by law. Take the item back to where you bought it, and explain clearly what happened, stating that it is not satisfactory and setting out what you want done about it. Very often the gunshop will be able to replace the item on the spot, or perhaps send it back to the manufacturer to be repaired free of charge under the warranty. It is important to do something about it straight away, rather than waiting several weeks before getting round to taking it back. The longer you leave it, the less likely you are to achieve a satisfactory result.

If the gunshop or manufacturer refuses to put the problem right, then you will have to enlist the help of someone who can assist you in forcing them to carry out their legal obligations. Your first stop is the Citizens' Advice Bureau – you will find their number in your 'phone book. They will be able to advise you on the merits of your case, and explain how to pursue the matter, through the courts if necessary. The County Courts now have a system known as the Small Claims Procedure, which allows you to bring a court action against a shop or company without going to the expense of hiring a solicitor. You can obtain a booklet explaining how to take such an action from the County Court, and once again the number is in your 'phone book. The threat of court action will often make your adversary see sense and straighten things out, but if you have to go to court it will help enormously if you have a written record of anything that has happened, including your receipt for the money you paid, a copy of any advertisement, copies of any letters you have sent and received, and preferably an independent expert's assessment of the fault. Bear this in mind whenever you buy something, and always keep copies of your receipts and letters.

There are special laws covering mail order, and most magazine publishers also belong to the Mail Order Protection Scheme, which provides compensation if you are unfortunate enough to be the victim of an unscrupulous mail order advertiser. One point worth remembering is that you have added protection if you buy something by mail order with a credit card such as Access or Barclaycard, because you can actually claim the money back from the credit card company if you cannot get satisfaction from the advertiser.

Please don't get the idea that manufacturers and gunshops are out to rip you off. The vast majority are proud of their reputation, and would do all in their power to make sure that you are a satisfied customer. But if you should run into problems, remember that the law is on your side. It's there to protect you, and there are advisory services who will help to see that justice is done.

Section II

AIRGUN HUNTING

15. Man the hunter

Those of us who enjoy hunting live quarry are all too familiar with the rhetorical question 'How *could* you kill poor little rabbits that haven't done anyone any harm?' The tone of the question implies that even to contemplate such a horrific act requires you to be in some way sub-human. The questioner assumes that no normal civilized human being could do such a thing, and those who do ought to be locked up to protect the innocent.

Not so long ago such a question would not have entered anyone's head. Life and death were a necessary part of man's existence. You were born, you took part in the harvesting of nature's resources which fed and clothed you, and when your turn came, you died. Death has become something of a taboo subject for modern man, however. A large proportion of the population is brought up in towns where milk comes out of bottles and clothes are something that you buy in Marks & Spencers. The countryside is where you drive to at the weekends for picnics, and where the farmers are nasty, greedy people who spray chemicals on the fields and keep chickens in biscuit boxes. How on earth do you explain the ethics of shooting live quarry to people like these?

Man was a hunting animal for thousands of years. By learning to till the fields and tend animals, he has been able to settle in one place and give up the nomadic existence that is necessary when you live by foraging from what nature provides. Modern civilization is based on the assumption that man has the right to manage nature to his own ends. We kill weeds and plant crops. We control pests and diseases, and grow animals for food. If we didn't, we would be reduced to wandering around prehistoric forests scavenging for food, and allowing ourselves to be eaten by wolves and bears. Fortunately – or unfortunately, depending on your viewpoint – we have come so far that it is perfectly possible to live your entire life without ever killing another creature with your own hands, although most people would squash a wasp on the window pane or poison a rat that moved into the house. But even if you never killed an animal in your life, if you were honest you would have to admit that other people were doing so on your behalf. But in today's society, every one of us has a choice. No one forces you to go out with an airgun and shoot a rabbit. You are free to sit at home and plink at tin cans, or watch the television. Yet thousands of people deliberately go out in search of live creatures to kill them. Why? And do we have a right to enjoy it?

It is easy enough to answer the question why. It is enjoyable, and a challenge. Hunting live quarry brings you closer to nature, and pits your skill and wits against the quarry in its own environment. There is great satisfaction to be had in outwitting your quarry, and concluding a painstaking stalk with a well aimed shot which kills the target instantly. Quite apart from the thrill of the stalk, and the satisfaction of a job well done, you can also be content in the knowledge that you have done the farmer a service by helping to control a pest which would have damaged crops intended for human consumption. But at the back of your mind, there may lurk a certain feeling of guilt – a sense of doubt about whether or not it is wrong to enjoy taking another creature's life. I have long since come to terms with this guilt. The fact is that we are not machines. We are living creatures which have evolved over millions of years, with emotions and urges which were designed to ensure the survival of our species in the natural world. We feel hunger, and eating satisfies us. We take pleasure in the act of reproduction. And there is a thrill that comes from the hunt which is so deep-rooted that no amount of civilization can totally hide it. By enjoying hunting, and admitting it, you are simply being true to yourself, and accepting what you are instead of pretending to be something else. Add that to the basic fact that man must kill in order to live, and you have to agree that hunting is an acceptable thing to do.

What is unacceptable is causing suffering. It is one thing to kill a creature quickly and cleanly; it is quite another to injure it and leave it to die slowly and in pain. We owe it to our quarry to do everything we can to ensure a quick, clean kill – and that goes for vermin just as much as game species. A rat may have some nasty habits, but it knows no better, and its behaviour does not provide an excuse for us to treat it with any less respect than any other creature. Before you go hunting, you should make sure that your equipment and your own skills are up to scratch, and never take a shot which might cause your quarry to suffer. Save the long-range, chancy shots for inanimate targets.

This principle of respecting your quarry is important. We have a natural tendency to justify what we are doing by criticising the creatures that we hunt. You see this in many other aspects of life as well as hunting. In wartime, the enemy is made out to be evil and depraved, as if that somehow justified blowing him to smithereens. Children in a playground will pick on the weakest, shyest one amongst them, like ducks on a pond that turn on one that is injured. Think of any example of man's inhumanity to man, and somewhere along the line those handing out the ill-treatment will have justified their actions by portraying their victims as inferior yet dangerous. Likewise, there is a tendency for airgunners to take the line that vermin such as rats and magpies have somehow deserved all they get and more. You see this coming out in some of the articles in airgun magazines, and in the way airgunners talk about their exploits. Creatures behave in the only way they know how, and they certainly do not deserve some sort of punishment for doing so. If you take the trouble to learn more about your quarry, you will be amazed at how well they have become adapted to their environment, and respect them for it. We may take a dim view of rats, but they do not go to war with one another, or plant bombs on civilian aeroplanes to further some political purpose. Next time you have a rat in your sights, ask yourself who has the stronger case for exterminating whom. Taking this theme a stage further, remember that vermin, like weeds, only need to be controlled where they are not wanted. Squirrels may be a serious pest in a forest, but where's the point in killing squirrels in your back garden? If you are killing a creature for food, then that is a different matter, but if you are killing it because it is vermin, make sure that your action is actually beneficial.

Sooner or later, you will come across someone who points out the apparent contradiction of claiming to be in favour of conservation, while you actually go out and kill wild creatures. How can the two be reconciled? In fact, the answer is quite simple. People who really understand the natural world realise that it is populations, rather than individuals of a species, that really matter. No one would seriously like to make rabbits extinct, despite what a farmer might say in a moment of desparation. But killing an individual rabbit does not bring extinction any closer. It simply helps to control the local population. True sportsmen would do all they could to prevent a species becoming extinct, but that does not prevent them from managing the population on a local level to allow man to live alongside. Nature is no lover of individuals, either. For the birds and animals in Britain's countryside, life is harsh. Many creatures have nothing better to look forward to than a lingering death by disease or starvation. Not at all the picture book world in some people's imagination, which leads to comments such as 'I don't know how you could be so cruel as to shoot a poor little bunny'. Cruelty is a difficult subject, anyway. To my mind, cruelty is chaining up a dog without food or water, or leaving it in a car on a baking hot summer's day. But where is the cruelty in killing a rabbit instantly with a pellet through its brain? Cruelty implies suffering, and the rabbit doesn't suffer for an instant. Death is a fact of life, and for us humans the suffering surrounding death is largely due to our understanding of death's finality. I don't believe a rabbit runs because it is afraid to die. It runs because its instinct tells it to, and fear is a part of that instinct. As soon as the threat has gone, the rabbit forgets its fear and goes back to its normal business of feeding and sleeping. If I walk through a field and startle a rabbit, am I not causing it more distress than if I had shot it cleanly?

You could argue the toss until the cows come home, and even then you would never reach agreement with those people who believe that shooting is wrong. I cannot say who is right and who is wrong. I do know that I feel satisfied in my own mind that there is nothing wrong in hunting and enjoying it – and that's what really matters. There are thousands of decent, honest, thoughtful people who feel the same way, and they cannot all be raving monsters.

I am not going to apologise for going into this subject in such detail. Life is the most precious thing we have, and you should never take a life lightly. Before you go hunting, you should think through the arguments on either side, and make quite sure that you believe what you are doing is right. Otherwise you are no better than the vermin you set out to control. If you remember nothing else from this chapter, remember this: your quarry deserves your respect; show a little humility, and do not fall into the trap of feeling that as a human being you are somehow superior to your quarry. In many ways, the birds and animals we hunt could teach us a thing or two!

16. Airgun quarry

If you are going to succeed at airgun hunting, you must first understand your quarry. Knowing the quarry's habits, needs and preferences will allow you to predict where you are likely to find it on any given day, and give you the best chance of filling the bag. You also need to know which senses the quarry species relies on to warn of danger, since this will help you to get within range without alarming it. In this chapter, we will look in turn at each of the main airgun quarry species, and highlight some of the most important facts about them. There is obviously a great deal more to learn than I can possibly include here, and some of it only comes with practice. For instance, I can tell at a glance whether a bird in flight is a woodpigeon, a collared dove or a racing pigeon, just by the way it flies – but I couldn't begin to put that into words. You can learn just so much from books, but there is no substitute for getting out into the countryside and learning from the best teacher of all, experience.

WOODPIGEON

The woodpigeon is familiar to just about everyone, even those who live in the centre of towns, because you find it even in the parks in the middle of London. It is one of those birds, like the house sparrow, which can adapt astonishingly well to many different kinds of environment. Partly for this reason, it is one of the most serious agricultural pests. The woodpigeon is a gregarious bird, meaning that it tends to congregate in flocks, which will converge on a field of young oilseed rape and strip it bare in no time. During the winter, a pigeon must eat a large amount of food just to keep alive, and this is also the time when many crop plants are at their most vulnerable stage. Since oilseed rape became more popular among Britain's farmers, the pigeon has become if anything even more of a pest, due to the terrible damage it can do to the crop during the winter months.

Pigeons are birds of habit. They like to roost in the same wood each night, and follow regular flight-lines to their feeding grounds. You should spend some time watching them to see where their roosts and feeding areas are, and which flight-lines

The woodpigeon has tough outer feathers which can be difficult for an airgun pellet to penetrate.

they follow between the two. They will also have their favourite trees which they use as look-out posts before swooping down to feed. All these places offer different opportunities for you to get a shot at the birds. You can wait for them as they come in to roost, and shoot them in the trees, although shooting upwards is difficult because the birds's heads are often hidden, and a shot in the well-muscled breast will not kill them. On the feeding ground is probably the best place, and it has the extra attraction that you will help to protect the crop by not allowing the birds to settle and feed. Stalking pigeons is very difficult because their eyesight is excellent, and the simplest way to shoot them is to find where they are feeding and build a good hide where you can lie in wait. Decoys will be a great help, because the birds like to feed in flocks and will be attracted to the decoys – although you must set the decoys out properly so that they look realistic. Set out as many decoys as you can lay your hands on, a few feet apart on the ground where they look as though they are feeding. If there is any wind, they should be facing into it, because a real pigeon would not feed with its back to the wind. A few decoy birds set up high on fenceposts or in trees will help to add realism to the scene, and you may even consider buying a 'flapper' cradle. This is a wire frame into which you place a dead bird (first shoot your pigeon!) A string leads from the cradle to your hide, and when you pull it the bird's wings flap. To a pigeon, this looks like a bird coming in to land, and it can help to attract birds to your decoys. Decoying pigeon is not as simple as it sounds, and there will be days when the birds will give even the best laid out decoy pattern a wide berth – especially if they have become accustomed to being shot over decoys.

When a pigeon comes in to land, it will sit upright for a few moments and look around before getting down to feeding. It is difficult for the bird to check out its surroundings thoroughly as it lands, so it wants to make sure it is safe first. While it is looking around, you must stay completely still, because it will spot the slightest movement. Once its head has gone down, you can slowly begin to bring the gun into position, but freeze if it raises its head again – this means that something has worried it and it is looking for signs of danger.

Pigeons have a notoriously tough layer of feathers, which will take a lot of the punch out of your pellet. For this reason, there is only one place to hit a pigeon for a clean kill – in the head. The head is a tiny target, only an inch or so across, and it will often be bobbing up and down as the bird feeds. But at least by aiming at the head you can be sure of either a clean kill or a clean miss and that is what you should always try to achieve when hunting.

COLLARED DOVE   The collared dove is a member of the same family as the pigeon, and has a similar appearance. Collared doves are lighter and more sandy in colour, smaller than a woodpigeon, and tend to frequent barns and other farm buildings rather than the fields and woods. Their name comes from the dark collar around the bird's neck, in place of the woodpigeon's white ring.

Living around the farmyard, collared doves feed on the grain in the store, especially any that has been spilled on the ground. They will sit on top of barns and on telephone wires overlooking the farm yard, waiting their moment to swoop. When disturbed, they tend not to go far, and soon return.

Not many years ago, collared doves were a rare sight in Britain, but recently they have become very common, and have been added to the list of quarry species. In many cases they do little harm and do not need to be controlled, but where they are able to get at the grain in the store, they will eat a significant amount, and spoil even more with their droppings.

Shooting collared doves is a relatively simple matter. They are used to people coming and going in the farmyard, and the buildings and machinery provide plenty of cover for you to hide. Position yourself so you have a good view of their favourite resting places – often a barn roof – and wait for them to return. Try to shoot when there are only one or two birds in the vicinity, because the noise of the shots will make the survivors more wary.

Unlike a pigeon, the collared dove's feathers are soft and provide little protection against an airgun pellet. Its body is lighter and more vulnerable, too, and a shot in the upper part of the body will give a clean kill. Do not allow your pellet to stray too low on the bird's chest, though, otherwise you will hit the large breast muscles instead of the vital heart/lung area.

RABBIT

Of all the airgun quarry, rabbits are probably the most popular. They are a common agricultural pest, are challenging to stalk, can be killed cleanly with a well-placed shot, and are delicious to eat. The outbreak of myxomatosis in the 1950s killed rabbits in their millions, and for several years it was thought that they might die out altogether. There are signs that strains of rabbits have now developed which are resistant to the disease, however, and they are rapidly building back up to their former numbers – and once again vying for the title of farmer's enemy number one. There can hardly be a farm in the country which now does not need to control rabbits.

Through the years, man has developed many different ways of killing rabbits: trapping, ferreting, snaring, long netting, coursing them with dogs, gassing them in their burrows, and of course shooting. It is probably true to say that you can never control rabbits completely with one method alone. You need to use a combination of two or more methods to keep them in check, but shooting with an airgun can be very effective.

Rabbits tend to stay in their burrows during the day, coming out at dusk to feed and going back underground soon after dawn. For this reason, a good scope is virtually essential for rabbit shooting, because you will stand the best chance of filling the bag when the light is poor. You can shoot rabbits successfully from a hide, but stalking is usually preferable. In a hide, you can only cover the rabbits in one burrow, and once you have fired the first shot the other rabbits in the burrow will be reluctant to come out. If you are stalking you can move around, taking one or two rabbits from each burrow in a wide area before returning to the first, by which time the remaining bunnies should have forgotten the original disturbance.

Rabbit shooting can be difficult in the early summer, when the grass is high and the quarry can feed without being spotted. At this time of year, it is best to concentrate on the more heavily grazed pastures, where you can see your quarry clearly. The chalk downland close to where I live is ideal, because the grass is kept cropped short by sheep all year round. Once the crops have been harvested, however, you can stalk rabbits very successfully on the stubbles, where they will sit out in the late summer sunshine. Rabbits seem to be able to forecast bad weather, because they will often come out in much greater numbers when there is a storm on the way. Presumably they want to fill their bellies before sitting out the storm underground. Rabbits can be very difficult to stalk because all their senses are highly developed. Their hearing and sense of smell are particularly good, but they will also spot a movement or a silhouette against the skyline.

The rabbit – probably the most popular airgun quarry.

Another method of rabbit shooting with an airgun is lamping, that is using a powerful spotlight at night. You can buy specially made rabbit lamping lights, which usually work from a rechargeable battery such as a motorcycle battery. If there are two of you, one can operate the lamp while the other shoots, or you can fit the lamp to your gun or a strap on your head. When a rabbit is caught in the beam, it will often freeze, not knowing which way to turn. This gives you the opportunity for a shot, but you must be quick because the rabbit will bolt sooner or later. One point to remember about lamping is that the law is very complicated on this subject, and you should check the legal position for your area before setting out. In some places lamping is illegal in any circumstances; in others you may only go lamping if you are the landowner. Make sure you do not break the law, and if there is anyone who might be concerned at seeing a light in the fields at night – such as a gamekeeper – tell them what you are doing beforehand.

GREY SQUIRREL

The grey squirrel is a common visitor to gardens in towns and villages, where it does little harm apart from taking the food put out for the birds, and occasionally breaking into tit nesting boxes to steal the eggs. But in the countryside, it can be a serious problem for foresters because it will chew the bark off young saplings and kill them. The grey squirrel is no friend of the gamekeeper's, either, because it eats grain put out for the pheasants, and raids game birds' nests. Do not confuse the grey squirrel with its relatively harmless cousin, the red squirrel. Red squirrels are quite rare in this country, and are protected. You can easily identify the red variety by their rusty red-brown colour, and large ear tufts.

Contrary to popular opinion, squirrels do not hibernate right through the winter, and you can find them searching for food even in the coldest months of the year. However, during the winter they do spend much more time in their dreys – spherical nests made of twigs and leaves which they build in tall trees. One way to control squirrels is to shake them from their dreys, and shoot them before they can run for cover. The normal time of year for this is February, when you are most likely to find the squirrels at home. If the drey is in a thin tree, you can simply shake the trunk until the occupants emerge, but in more sturdy trees you will need a long pole to poke the drey. The type of poles sold for lofting pigeon decoys are ideal, because they come in light sections of hollow tube about six feet long, which are easy to carry and can be assembled to give sufficient length. You

The grey squirrel – a serious pest in forests, and where game birds are reared.

can shoot many squirrels in a day by this method using a shotgun, but with an airgun it is more difficult because they will often emerge from the drey running at full tilt. All you can do then is try to out-run them on the ground and get ahead of them – and hope your quarry will stop when you face it.

Even when they have not been disturbed from their dreys, squirrels are often difficult to shoot in trees because they are so agile and move so fast through the branches. If possible, it is often better to bait a spot with grain for a week or two, and then lie in wait for the squirrels as they come to feed.

A squirrel's skin is very tough, and you must achieve a good hit to kill one cleanly. Aim for the head or the upper part of the chest, and don't be tempted to shoot at any other part of the animal if the 'kill zones' are hidden from view by a branch. If a squirrel knows that you are down below, it will often freeze against a branch on the opposite side, so you cannot get a clear shot. If this happens you must try to manoeuvre so you can see its head or chest, although it will often move round as you do to keep the branch between you. If you are shooting with a companion, you can split up and walk round opposite sides, forcing the squirrel to show itself. If you are alone, however, you can sometimes confuse a squirrel by throwing a stick or even your coat to the opposite side of the tree.

BROWN RAT

Like the rabbit, the rat is a favourite airgun quarry. Even the most ardent anti is unlikely to mind people shooting rats, such is the loathing that man has for the creatures. Much of this hatred stems from fear, and few animals instil such fear into man for no good reason. There are countless stories of the exploits of rats, including a good many far-fetched tales involving the supernatural! Quite apart from this, rats are a terrible pest in food stores and livestock buildings, and spread various diseases such as leptospirosis. If you should ever be unfortunate – or foolish – enough to be bitten by a rat, you should seek medical advice immediately. In fact, it is not a good idea even to handle a dead rat, and you should wash your hands thoroughly after touching them or anywhere they have been.

Rats generally live in the fields during the summer months, and move into the farm buildings as the cold weather approaches. Even out in the fields they cause problems, taking eggs and young birds, and eating grain intended for game. Once in the farm buildings, they will damage far more than they eat, even chewing through electrical cables and wooden joists. Rats feed at night, and it is after dark that you stand the best chance of shooting them. Find out where they are feeding, and wait quietly out of sight. You will often hear them before you see them, because they tend to scuffle along.

I have had great success shooting rats on feed rides where the gamekeeper puts down food for the pheasants. The rats soon learn the keeper's routine, and will be waiting close by when he arrives for the regular feed. Let him spread the food as usual, then wait for the rats to appear after he has gone. Very often the first rats will be out as soon as his back is turned. Don't bother collecting the dead bodies until you have finished shooting. The other rats do not seem to be alarmed by the corpses, but they will however be scared off if you keep walking up and down.

Around farm buildings and grain stores, you can often leave a light on to give you sufficient light to shoot by, although it can be a good idea to replace the normal bright bulb with a low powered one.

Rats are quite easy to kill with an airgun, and a good hit almost anywhere in the upper part of the body will kill them instantly. There is no need to aim for the head; go for the chest, lining up the cross-hairs on the shoulder. Some people prefer to use .25 calibre for rat shooting because of its greater stopping power. There is no doubt that a .25 pellet will knock a rat clean off its feet, but I have never had any problems using .22 or even .177. I do like to use flat-headed pellets for rats, however, because a pointed pellet can easily pass straight through the soft body of a rat, without transmitting all of its power on the way.

CROW

There are two types of crow in Britain: the carrion crow and the hooded crow. They are virtually identical except that the carrion crow is all black, whereas the hooded crow has a grey 'saddle' across its back. The carrion crow is found in the south of Britain, and the 'hoodie' in the north and Scotland. Crows are a great enemy of livestock. They will attack mercilessly any animal that is sick or injured and unable to defend itself, and frequently peck out the eyes and tongue of new-born lambs. For this reason, they are controlled vigorously in livestock farming areas, and they are also a menace to game birds so gamekeepers are pleased to see them shot, too.

Crows are loners, living either singly or in pairs, and do not normally flock together. They are also extremely wary, with excellent eyesight, making them very difficult to shoot with a

Carrion crows – a very tricky quarry to stalk.

shotgun, never mind an air rifle. They do not follow regular patterns of behaviour, so there is little scope for shooting them at roosting places. You can sometimes shoot them at the nest, but you should make sure that you don't leave any chicks in the nest to starve. The other way to get to grips with crows is setting a bait to attract them – a dead rabbit can be effective. Build a hide that will keep you covered from all directions, including directly above. Then set out the bait where you can get a clear shot, and wait. The problem is that you can wait a long time without results, and you must be very patient.

The hooded crow is identical to the carrion crow except for the grey patches on its body.

A crow is a big, strong bird, and to kill it with an airgun you really need to hit it in the head. This can be difficult when it is feeding, because it will be pecking away at the food and the head will rarely be still. Wait until the bird stops to look around before taking the shot.

ROOK

Rooks are often confused with crows, because they look quite similar. They are smaller, however, and have a white patch at the base of the beak. Rooks live and feed in flocks, and there is a lot of truth in the saying 'If you see a lot of crows together, they are rooks; if you see a rook on its own, it's a crow'. They nest in rookeries – a collection of nests close together in tall trees.

In days gone by, rooks were shot for food, but nowadays few

WHICH TYPE OF GUN?

Your next decision is whether to buy a spring-powered gun or a pneumatic. If it's a spring gun, do you want the fixed barrel or break-barrel type? If you choose a pneumatic, you must decide whether to go for a pump-up or the type you charge up from an air cylinder. The pros and cons of the various types were covered in Chapter 3. Personally, I prefer a spring-powered gun of the break-barrel type, but there are many hunters more experienced than me who choose one of the other types. It is really a matter for personal preference, but do bear in mind whether or not you will be using the gun away from home for long periods, when you are on holiday for instance, and whether you might want to take several shots in quick succession. Perhaps you will want to use the same gun for field target shooting, in which case this will influence your choice, too.

You have probably noticed that I have carefully avoided giving a shopping list of 'recommended' guns. This is because it would be unfair to name just a few, when there are so many excellent guns around – and in any case, any guns I named would be only my own personal favourites. Another person might list completely different guns, and who is to say which of us would be right? One word of advice, though – or is it a plea from the heart? Don't let people tell you that foreign guns are always best. There are some excellent British guns which are just as good as, if not better than, anything the Germans, Japanese and the rest can offer. I hope that somewhere along the line, you will at least give the British gunmakers a fair crack of the whip in your selection.

Before you get too carried away with fancy woodwork and highly polished brass fittings, remember what you are buying the gun for. More often than not, you will be crawling around in a muddy ditch, up to your neck in thorns and brambles. You won't want to be concerned about protecting the stock in a situation like that. And those shiny brass plates and mounts may look good in the gun rack, but out in the field they will serve only to flash a warning to your quarry. A hunting rifle is a working tool. It should do its job efficiently without getting in the way. You wouldn't dig the garden with a gold plated spade. It makes a lot more sense to spend an extra few pounds on tuning, or a better scope and mounts, rather than things which improve the gun's appearance.

MAKING YOUR FINAL SELECTION

By this stage, you should have narrowed your choice down to just two or three possible guns, and this is the time to ask your friends, or even the man in the gunshop, whether you can try out the guns to make your final selection. Just a few shots will help enormously in making up your mind. Use a proper target and try to shoot a really tight group. Never mind whether or not the gun is zeroed – you can deal with that later. You may find that for no apparent reason you can shoot a tighter group with one gun than with another. For various reasons, some people find they can shoot more accurately with one particular gun, and if so, then that's the one to choose. Alternatively, you may simply find that one gun feels more comfortable to shoot, or the stock fits you better. All these things will influence your choice.

There is still one important decision to be made: what calibre do you want? If you can't make up your mind, then you may like to go back and read Chapter 9, where I set out the advantages and disadvantages of the main airgun calibres. For my money, I would go for .177 every time. It has no shortage of stopping power, and the flatter trajectory makes it easier to hit the target.

When you have finally reached your decision, please be fair to your local gunsmith. If he has helped you with your choice, and taken the trouble to show you various guns, don't just walk out of the shop and buy the gun from wherever you can get the cheapest price. Gunsmiths don't live on fresh air, and if you do him out of a sale you may find that, when you next want advice, he isn't so co-operative – or even that he has gone out of business and isn't there any more. If you know what gun you want, by all means find the cheapest price, but don't treat your gunsmith as a free advice service.

ACCESSORIES FOR YOUR GUN

Let's assume you have now bought your gun, and you're itching to get out into the fields and try it out. You aren't ready yet, of course, because there are several other bits and pieces that you need before you are properly kitted out for hunting. First of all, you will probably want a scope and mounts. As with the gun, this is a matter of deciding on the specification you want, and then looking at what is available in your price bracket. You will find the choice narrowing down as you learn more about what's available. And just as you did with the gun, you should try out the scopes on your short-list before reaching a decision.

You may want to add various extras to your gun besides a scope. A sling can be very helpful, making it easier to carry the gun in the field as well as steadying your aim. A silencer is also a good idea, because it will reduce the disturbance you make when you are shooting and increase your chances of coming across other quarry nearby. A pellet holder can be fitted to the

A scarf wrapped round the gun to camouflage it must be kept clear of parts such as the trigger and breech.

gun's stock to keep your pellets handy but out of harm's way, and you may also want to camouflage the gun with pieces of scrim or a special DPM sleeve. Camouflage should only be fitted as a temporary measure, however, because you will need to remove it after shooting in damp conditions so that you can clean the gun and allow it to dry out properly without danger of rusting.

HUNTING PELLETS

Your choice of hunting pellets is important. Some people carry different pellets for different quarry, but I believe this causes confusion. Instead of remembering one trajectory, you must remember one for each type of pellet, and in the heat of the moment you may get muddled up between them. It is far better in my opinion to choose one pellet that will perform adequately in every situation. My own preference is for the flat-headed type, but many hunters swear by the old-fashioned roundheads such as the Eley Wasp. Certainly these pellets must have accounted for more quarry in the bag over the years than all the other types put together, and if you can put them in the right place they will do a first-class job of stopping the quarry whether it is bird or animal, large or small.

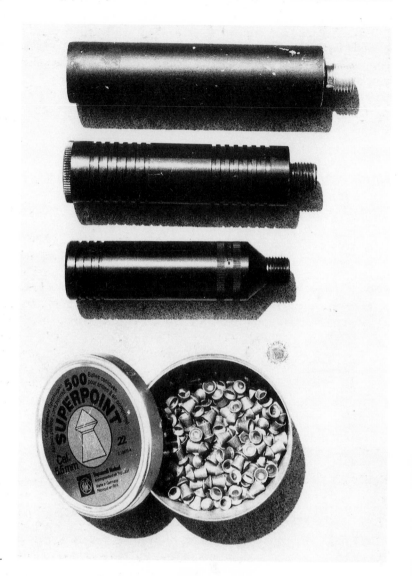

Three types of air-
gun silencer, with a
tin of RWS Super-
point pellets to
show their size.

18. Clothing and equipment

As any experienced hunter will tell you, the clothing you wear for hunting is very important. It must protect you from the elements, and also help you to remain unobserved by your quarry.

If you are going to hunt seriously, you will find yourself outside in all extremes of weather, and even a warm day can quickly turn nasty. Every year you hear of people who are caught out on the hills and moors of Britain by a sudden change of weather, and die of exposure because they are not adequately protected. Shooting in a cornfield on a lowland farm may seem a million miles from the bleak hillsides of Snowdonia or the Peak District, but you can still feel very uncomfortable if you aren't properly protected. The worst combination is wet and wind together. Even on a hot summer's day, you will feel chilly if you wear a wet shirt and stand in the wind. At the other extreme, the 'chill factor' caused by a 70 km/hr wind can make 0 degrees centigrade feel like minus 20!

KEEPING WARM

Good outdoor clothing needs to keep you warm and dry without restricting your movements more than necessary. The best method is to build up your clothing in layers. Several thin layers of clothing are warmer than one or two thick ones, because the layers of air trapped between them insulate your body from the cold outside. Trapped air is the best insulator, which is why a string vest keeps you warm even though it is full of holes. Wearing several thin layers also allows you more flexibility because you can discard layers as necessary if the weather becomes warmer, or if you generate heat by walking around. A waterproof and windproof outer layer will keep the weather out, allowing the inner layers to do their job properly.

For hide shooting in winter, my first layer is thermal long johns and a long-sleeved vest. The second layer is moleskin trousers and a warm shirt. Then I add a woollen jumper and quilted bodywarmer to the top half of my body. And finally I put proofed cotton camouflage trousers and a camouflage jacket over the top. Insulated wellington boots with two layers of thin woollen socks keep my feet warm, and a balaclava helmet keeps the wind off my face. If the weather is very wet, I might use a waxed cotton Barbour jacket, waterproof trousers and a hat instead of the camouflage gear. You can now buy waxed cotton jackets in a camouflage pattern, which makes them more suitable for airgun hunting than the more familiar plain dark greens and browns favoured by game shooters.

This is the warmest clothing I have found which still allows you to move enough to shoot properly. If I need to move around, or the weather improves, it is a simple matter to take off a layer or two – the quilted bodywarmer and the moleskin trousers, for instance. This system also saves you money, because you don't need to buy different jackets and trousers for shooting at different times of the year. In summer, you can wear the same cotton camouflage jacket and trousers, with just light underwear beneath.

FOOTWEAR

Footwear for hunting is a matter for personal choice, but it goes without saying that it should be stout enough to stand up to heavy use. Wellingtons are virtually essential in wet weather or snow, and if you suffer from cold feet you may prefer the insulated variety, or even the 'moon boot' type with thick foam insulation if you are going to be stationary in a hide for long periods. In better weather, and for stalking, lighter shoes or boots may be preferable. Leather boots with 'commando' type soles are very good and give plenty of protection, but I like to use light trainers or tennis shoes in the summer. These are more comfortable and allow your feet to breathe, and the soles are also thin enough to allow you to feel the ground beneath you before you put your weight down fully. This means you can feel a twig under your foot and avoid snapping it which would make a noise and alarm your quarry. Light shoes like these are not made for such heavy use, however, and a pair will only last you one season before they are fit for the dustbin.

CAMOUFLAGE

You will have noticed that, in every case, I am using a camouflaged outer layer. Camouflage is very important for airgun hunting because to shoot live quarry effectively with an airgun you need to get quite close without alarming it, so you have time to aim properly and shoot at a stationary target. Game shooters using shotguns do not have to worry so much about being spotted by their quarry, since they can shoot it on the move.

Good camouflage is quite an art, and to be effective you must not only camouflage yourself properly but also use it well. That means avoiding unnecessary movement, for instance, and taking care not to be silhouetted against a very light or very dark background – but more of that in the next chapter.

There are many different types of camouflage clothing, and choosing between them can be difficult. Which one of the various patterns will be most effective, bearing in mind the type of terrain in which you will be hunting?

All camouflage works on the same basic principle. It confuses the eye, and breaks up the easily recognised human outline. To do this, it must blend in with the surroundings, with a random pattern of natural colours arranged so that the eye doesn't see a

The British Army style DPM is the best type of camouflage – this outfit is made by Teal Countrywear.

clear line where the camouflage stops and the natural foliage begins.

Some types of camouflage do not have sufficient contrast between the darker and lighter patches, so you can still see the outline of the clothing against a natural background. Others have too much contrast, with very dark and very light patches which themselves look unnatural. The best camouflage to my mind is the British Army DPM (disruptive pattern material) design, which strikes just the right balance and is ideally suited to the type of foliage that you find in Britain. This is hardly surprising, because a solider's needs are very similar to those of an airgun hunter: he must see without being seen, while remaining warm and comfortable so he can operate effectively. This explains why ex-Army gear is so popular with airgunners, although there is now plenty of clothing using the Army style DPM which is designed specially for airgun hunting. Even this excellent material is a little on the dark side when it is brand new, but it fades and becomes more effective with age. When I buy a new camouflage jacket or pair of trousers, I put them through the washing machine a few times before using them in the field. This tends to remove the waterproofing compounds from the cloth, though, so you may need to re-proof them with one of the proprietary sprays to give good protection.

One of the advantages of the light cotton material used in these clothes is that it dries very quickly. A light shower will not penetrate the material, but heavy rain will find its way through eventually, even if the material is proofed. The material is sufficiently windproof that it will not feel too cold even when wet, and an hour or two in the sun will soon dry it out again. It does become significantly darker when wet, which makes it less effective, however. For real protection against rain, there is nothing to beat the waxed cotton used by manufacturers such as Barbour, and if you are going to spend any length of time out of doors in bad weather a well-made waxed cotton coat and trousers are a good investment. These are now available in DPM-type camouflage material, although the colours are not quite so good as those in the standard cotton material. Waxed cotton is also rather stiffer than ordinary cotton, so your freedom of movement is a little restricted – but that's a small sacrifice compared to the misery of spending a day out of doors soaked to the skin!

FEATURES OF GOOD HUNTING CLOTHES

Whatever type of jacket and trousers you use, the design will be important as well as the type of material. Look for good, strong zips and fasteners, and plenty of deep pockets for carrying all the bits and pieces you will need for a day's hunting. There should be a wide collar that you can turn up against the wind to protect your neck, a generous storm flap across the zip at the front, and cuffs which button up tight to keep the wind and rain out. Many modern jackets use Velcro fastening on the pockets, but I find this noisy and I prefer the simple poppers such as the ones you find on a Barbour jacket. Zips vary enormously, too, and only the strongest are really up to the job. Nylon zips run more smoothly when new, but a good metal zip will last longer and become more easy to operate as it breaks in. You can make a new metal zip run more smoothly by rubbing a wax candle against the teeth to lubricate it. Trouser zips, in particular, are often not really strong enough, so take a close look before you buy. Remember that you will be crawling through the undergrowth, and anything which sticks out will tend to catch on twigs and brambles. Epaulettes, for instance, may look smart, but they are always getting tangled up when you are stalking. The same goes for webbing straps and little pouches for pellets, knives and so on. I prefer to keep everything in my pockets, out of harm's way.

COMPLETING YOUR CAMOUFLAGE

Wearing a good camouflage jacket and trousers is only part of camouflaging yourself effectively, of course, because they only cover part of you. Your hands and face will stand out clearly against a natural background, so they need the camouflage treatment, too. The standard answer is to wear gloves or mittens on your hands, and a face veil or balaclava over your head. This will do the job effectively, and help to keep you warm in winter, but in summer it will be far too hot. The best answer is to use camouflage make-up, which you simply wipe onto your face and hands to give a camouflage pattern. This will leave your face and hands unrestricted, and is a lot more comfortable to wear. At the end of the day, you simply wash it off. You can buy camouflage make-up from specialist gunshops, or scrounge some make-up of the right colour from your local amateur dramatic society. Alternatively, some shops sell children's face paints, which do the job just as well. You will have to discard the bright reds, blues and yellows, or save them for your next fancy dress party, but that will leave you with a good selection of colours for a camouflage effect. One word of warning, though. Beware of using camouflage make-up if you are shooting in an area where you are likely to be seen by members of the public. Even game shooters find it difficult to appreciate why airgunners need to dress up in full camouflage, and they

Left: An alternative to purpose-made camouflage make-up – children's face paints.

Right: Applying camouflage make-up, with the aid of the Land-Rover's wing mirror.

are inclined to criticise airgun hunters for 'playing at soldiers'. Parading around in camouflage make-up will only confirm their prejudices, and do the sport no good at all.

As well as camouflaging yourself, it pays to camouflage your gun, too. The gun has a distinct outline and colours which show up as unnatural to a wary bird or animal. You can break up its outline, and eliminate reflections which could alarm the quarry, by wrapping it in scrim material such as that sold as scarves. You must keep the material loose so that the folds and creases form a disruptive pattern of different colours, and make sure that it won't get in the way and prevent you using the gun properly. Parts to keep clear include the breech, the sights, the muzzle, and the trigger – and you will find it easier to shoot comfortably if you keep the grip of the stock free of material, too. Alternatively, you can buy specially designed gun 'chaps' which are tailored to fit the gun precisely, and are made of camouflage material.

What else do you need for a day's hunting? The gun, scope and pellets were all dealt with in the previous chapter, but there are a few other items that will come in useful, although you could do without them at a pinch.

OTHER EQUIPMENT FOR HUNTING

The first of these is a good knife, which can come in handy for all sorts of jobs, from removing a thorn from your finger to cutting small branches to improve a hide. Many airgunners buy knives which are totally unsuitable for the job, however. The huge Rambo-style jungle knives with everything but the kitchen sink hidden in the handle are all very well if you are hunting elephants, but they are not much use for skinning a rabbit, for instance. They are bulky and heavy, and not delicate enough for most of the jobs that will arise when you are airgun hunting. Collecting knives can be great fun, but don't kid yourself that you need a huge knife for hunting. The best choice is a small pocket knife with a few simple tools built in – a Swiss Army knife with a saw blade, can opener and a couple of small blades is ideal. It will cope with all but the heaviest jobs, and slips easily into your pocket without getting in the way and catching on the undergrowth.

A length of string will take up virtually no room in a pocket, but can be very useful for all kinds of odd jobs. You can use it as a makeshift game bag to help you carry what you have shot, repair a broken bootlace, tie up your camouflage netting where there isn't a branch handy, and a hundred and one other things.

Sticking plasters are another small item which are no trouble to carry but can be very handy if you cut yourself or develop a

Binoculars with a camouflaged rubber armour finish.

blister, so it is well worth slipping a few in a pocket. Toilet paper falls into the same category. Laugh if you like, but he who laughs last . . . !

You can use your scope for spotting your quarry at a distance, but binoculars are easier to use and give a wider field of view. They do take up more room than some of your other equipment, however, so you may prefer to use the miniature type, or make do without them altogether. I use a pair of 8 x 30 Zeiss binoculars, which give a very sharp image and are powerful enough to show you much more than the naked eye can see. They are also fairly light and small, which is an advantage over the more powerful binoculars such as 10 x 50s. Some binoculars have rubber armour, similar to a rubber armoured scope, which can be an advantage in the field because it protects them against knocks and muffles the sound if they bump against your rifle.

A game bag can be useful, especially if you are taking a packed lunch with you as well as all the other equipment. If you just want something to carry what you shoot, a light net bag will slip into a pocket and hold a dozen rabbits or more if necessary. But for hide shooting, when you will want a vacuum flask, sandwiches, camouflage netting, and so on, a proper game bag is a good idea. The canvas type with a net pouch on the front will keep your food separate from dead quarry, and also makes a good waterproof seat – provided you remember to take out your sandwiches first!

There are many other bits and pieces which can add to a day in the countryside, whether you are hunting or just out for a walk. I usually take a camera, because I enjoy taking photos of wildlife and the countryside, and that involves a bag to carry spare film, lenses and so on. If I am shooting with a friend, I will often take a walkie-talkie radio, too. About a year ago I bought a pair of hand-held CB radios which have a range of a mile or two. They can be useful when hunting, because you can warn each other of approaching quarry, discuss tactics, or simply arrange where to meet for lunch. On a bad day, when you sit for long periods in a hide with no sign of your quarry, it certainly relieves the boredom to be able to chat to someone else while you wait.

I could go on for ever about the many different items which you could take with you, and if you took the lot you wouldn't be able to move under the weight. It doesn't matter so much when you are shooting from a hide, but do remember that for stalking everything you take will add to the weight you must carry with you all day, and by lunchtime you may be wishing you had left most of it behind.

19. In the field

Airguns do not have a very good reputation with the general public. The average man in the street thinks of airgunners as hooligans who go round taking pot shots at anything that moves – including the 7.45 to London and the neighbour's cat. Many country people share this opinion of airgunners, perhaps because they have never come across serious airgunners, but have read the horror stories which appear in the newspapers from time to time. In fact this is far from the true picture. The majority of airgunners are responsible people who respect their quarry and the countryside, while a minority bring the sport into disrepute.

But the fact remains that airgunners face a great deal of hostility from the public at large. That places an extra burden of responsibility on each and every one of us to behave properly. It isn't enough just to act responsibly. Airgunners must be seen to be responsible people. In the long run, this will determine whether or not we are free to enjoy our sport. It wouldn't take many bad reports in the press before a public outcry would force the government to introduce laws restricting the use of airguns, banning their use on live quarry, and bringing them under the same controls as firearms – and that would mean the end of our sport as we know it today.

THE THREAT TO FIELD SPORTS

In fact, all forms of field sports are constantly under attack from the 'antis', who would like to ban all field sports, starting with coursing and hunting, and going on to outlaw shooting and even fishing. On top of that, there is the anti-gun lobby, who feel that ordinary people like you and me are not fit to own and use guns. They believe that all weapons, from crossbows to deer rifles, should be tightly controlled. To back up their argument, they quote statistics showing the rise in armed crime – claiming that tighter restrictions would reduce the crime rate. Experience in other countries has shown that this doesn't work, but there is a great deal of public support for their argument, and every time a report appears in a newspaper about misuse of guns, their case gains a little more ground. What the papers don't report is the vast numbers of ordinary, decent people who go out every weekend and enjoy their sport responsibly, causing no trouble to anyone and helping the farmer by controlling pests. You can help by behaving sensibly when you go hunting. Don't give the antis any more ammunition to fire at us. Remember that many people are frightened of guns and don't understand them. They will be alarmed if you fire a shot and then jump out of a bush next to them camouflaged from head to toe. Never mind that you were firing at a rabbit in the opposite direction. They will go home and tell their friends how they were attacked by a mad gunman in the woods – and the antis will have another convert to their cause.

Join the BASC

Apart from behaving properly in the field, there is something else you can do to help protect your sport. Join the British Association for Shooting and Conservation, or BASC as they are usually known. This organisation represents all types of shooters, including airgun hunters, looking after their interests and standing up for them in parliament. Simply by being on their membership list, you add strength to their voice. The larger their membership, the more politicians will have to listen to what they say. By joining the BASC, you receive free insurance cover, legal advice, and a regular copy of the association's magazine, *Shooting and Conservation*. But the way I see it, all these are extra benefits. The real reason for joining is to add your support to the cause of shooting.

The BASC also publishes a Code of Practice for airgun shooting, which is full of good advice. But this Code of Practice only sets down the minimum standards that all airgunners should follow. In reality, you can – and should – go a great deal further. Some points are obvious, such as not littering the countryside and only shooting at legitimate quarry species. The country code is a good starting point. This covers the basic points such as keeping your dog under control, shutting gates behind you, not damaging crops, and so on. But the airgunner's code goes far beyond this. The airgunner has a responsibility not just to the farmer and his crops and livestock, but also to the countryside as a whole and the different creatures that live there.

Before you set out, you should discuss with the farmer or gamekeeper exactly what you can and cannot do. He may want you to keep away from certain woods because the pheasants are breeding, for instance, or he may ask that you don't shoot certain quarry species. He will certainly be able to tell you where the boundaries of the farm lie, so that you don't inadvertently stray off the land where you have a right to shoot, and he can also warn you of any footpaths which cross the land. You have a duty to respect his wishes, and not betray his trust. Quite apart from anything else, if you are caught misbehaving, you will certainly not be allowed to shoot there again.

Listen to the farmer, the gamekeeper, and anyone else who works and lives in the countryside. You never stop learning about the environment, and that is one of the great pleasures to be had from hunting. Shooting is not a numbers game. There are no prizes for killing the biggest bag, although we all enjoy a successful day from time to time. Very often, you will come home empty handed, but in high spirits because you have been privileged to see a rare creature, or learned a little more about the natural world. The days that stand out in my memory are not those when I made a big bag, but when I watched a stoat hunting a rabbit, or happened upon an adder basking in the sunshine.

In the field, I aim to leave no trace of my presence, like a shadow passing across the ground that leaves no mark once it has gone. This covers a whole range of 'don'ts': don't walk through growing crops, don't climb over fences and damage them, don't leave empty cans lying around, don't carve your initials into trees, don't do this, don't do that. But more importantly, it is an attitude of mind which will not only help to ensure that you are invited back to shoot there again, but also improve your chances of success.

UNDER- STANDING THE COUNTRYSIDE

The best hunters are those who really understand the country-side, and become a part of it. That goes a lot further than simply knowing your quarry. You need to understand the farmer's way of life. What crops is he growing and why? When are they sown, and when are they harvested? Can you tell the difference between wheat and barley, or even wheat and grass? By knowing the answers, you will gain much more pleasure from being in the fields, and you will also be able to plan your hunting better. For instance, you may know that such-and-such a crop is due to be harvested in the next few days, and you can expect to be able to stalk the rabbits in the stubble afterwards. Or perhaps you know that the farmer is growing oilseed rape in a certain field, making it a good bet for pigeon decoying when the snow falls.

You will remember from school biology lessons that plants,

animals, birds and insects all interact with one another by way of food chains. A magpie eats the eggs of a kestrel, which eats voles, which eat plants, which need nitrogen fixed in the soil by microscopic bugs. And when the magpie dies, it provides food for insects and bacteria . . . and so it goes on.

When you shoot a bird or animal, you don't just reduce the population of that species by one. Your action has an effect all the way down the food chain. Killing a single rabbit may have little effect on the environment as a whole, but if you eliminate all the rabbits in an area you will change the whole pattern of wildlife there.

The Game Conservancy's Cereals and Gamebirds Research Project, for instance, has shown how modern farming practices have contributed to the decline in numbers of partridges in Britain. By killing insects to protect their crops, farmers have taken away an important part of the diet of young partridge chicks. Now farmers are being encouraged to leave the edges of fields unsprayed, so that partridge chicks will have plenty of food and the birds can build up their numbers once again.

I was very impressed when I visited the Eskdalemuir Forest in the Scottish Borders. The wildlife manager there explained how the foresters had come to understand that they could not fight the forces of nature. Instead, they managed the wildlife in the forest to their own benefit. They built nestboxes for birds of prey, so that kestrels and owls would control the voles which gnaw at the young trees, for instance. And they planted areas of deciduous trees among the conifers to encourage small song-birds, because the small birds eat insects that damage the trees and spread disease.

What this comes down to is that you should never kill anything simply because it is on the list of legitimate quarry species. The fact that magpies are classified as vermin does not give you *carte blanche* to exterminate them. When you peer through the sights at a living creature, you hold its life in your hands, and the decision whether or not to pull the trigger has repercussions which go far beyond that one individual, like ripples spreading across a pond. In a small way, you are affecting the balance of nature, and that is not something that should be taken lightly.

20. The stalk

There are two basic ways of coming to terms with your quarry. You can sit and wait for it to come to you, or you can go in search of it and try to creep close enough for a shot. In this chapter we look at the latter method – stalking.

You could spend a fortune on the best air rifle, scope and camouflage gear, practise your marksmanship until you can hit a match-head at 20 yards, and have the shooting rights over land teeming with all kinds of quarry, but you still won't shoot a thing unless you can master the art of fieldcraft. A fox or cat is nowhere near so well camouflaged as a human hunter, and certainly not so well armed, but it knocks spots off even the most experienced airgunner when it comes to catching its quarry. The reason is simple. Wild animals are born with a natural instinct for fieldcraft. They can make themselves invisible in an instant, and stalk their prey so skilfully that they can approach near enough to pounce before they are spotted. To a human, these skills don't come naturally; they must be learned, and that takes plenty of practice. You can pick up the basic principles by reading about them, but there is no substitute for getting out into the field and learning from your mistakes.

KNOW YOUR QUARRY

The most important thing is to know your quarry, and understand what will alarm it. Quarry species are well used to being hunted, and they have become very skilled at keeping out of trouble. Their senses are highly developed, and at the slightest hint of danger they will make themselves scarce. If you go blundering into one end of a wood, snapping twigs and thumping your feet loudly on the ground, any quarry inside will have gone out of the other end long before you reach it, and you will go home wondering why there was nothing to be seen.

But quarry are only flesh and blood, and their senses are the same as ours: sight, hearing, smell, taste and touch. If you can avoid letting your quarry sense you in any of these ways, you will be able to get close enough for a shot. It's as simple – and difficult – as that. The problem is that your quarry's senses are so much more highly developed than a human's. A rabbit will hear a twig snap, catch a whiff of human scent, or feel a thud on the ground, which a human couldn't begin to detect. So you must be acutely aware of everything you do which might give yourself away. Don't forget that birds and animals all have their own distinctive alarm calls, which serve to warn all the other creatures around that there is danger about. If you alarm a blackbird, for example, its alarm call will alert your quarry just as effectively as if it had spotted you itself.

Sight

Let's deal with the quarry's senses one by one, taking sight first. Camouflage is one way in which you can help to remain unnoticed by your quarry. But even the best camouflage will only do its job if you use if properly. Some people behave as though wearing camouflage made them invisible, which quite obviously isn't the case. If you doubt that, just watch anyone wearing camouflage clothing as they walk across a field, or along the edge of a wood. You can see them quite clearly, despite the camouflage, even if they stand still. The problem is that camouflage is a compromise. The colours are too dark for some backgrounds, and too light for others. And against a plain background of any colour, the camouflage will stand out. The direction of the light plays an important role, too. When light falls on you, parts of you will be lit strongly, and others will be in shadow. This tends to highlight your shape, and make you stand out from the background, and the effect is most obvious in strong sunlight.

Even a small patch of nettles such as this can help to conceal you from your quarry.

You can help the camouflage to do its job by keeping out of strong sunlight, and in cover where the natural foliage tends to break up your outline anyway. You can demonstrate this with a simple experiment. Stand outside a wood, and ask a friend wearing camouflage to walk slowly into the wood away from you, a step or two at a time. At first, you will see him clearly, because his shape will stand out against the darker shade of the wood behind. As he moves back into the wood, he will become more and more difficult to see. You may know where he is, but you will not be able to make out his outline, and if he stands still you may lose him altogether. If you then ask him to lie down among the undergrowth, he will be even harder to spot. But even if you are wearing camouflage, he will still be able to see you clearly, because you will be silhouetted against the fields and sky behind. The lesson of all this is clear. Camouflage isn't effective unless you keep in the shade, with a certain amount of cover between you and your quarry, and avoid movement as much as possible. In short, you should behave as though you were wearing a bright orange boiler suit, even when you are camouflaged up to the eyeballs.

Sound

So much for sight, but what about sound? Most quarry birds and animals have a powerful sense of hearing which can pick up sounds way beyond the range of the human ear. The scuffing of your clothes as you walk, or the chink of metal, will alert them to danger just as much as the sight of you walking across a field towards them. Before you set off for a day's hunting, check over your clothes and equipment to see whether there is anything which might make a noise. Leave your loose change at home rather than carrying it in your pocket, and put sticky tape over any clips and buckles that might rattle. Most purpose-made hunting clothes are designed so that they do not make a noise when they rub together, and they tend not to have rattly zips and poppers. Nylon is a very noisy material, which is why most shooters prefer cotton. Bear all this in mind when you choose a jacket or trousers for hunting. Even your boots can make a noise. Some wellingtons have buckles at the top, for instance, and these can make a terrible noise as you walk. It's best to cut them off, or stick them down with insulating tape to keep them silent.

In the field, you must take care to avoid making a noise as you move. It is all too easy to step on a twig when you are concentrating on not being seen by your quarry, for instance, and even dead leaves can make enough noise to alarm a rabbit when you step on them. Before you put your foot down, check to see that there is nothing beneath it which could make a sudden noise. With practice, you can do this by feel rather than by looking down at each step, and it helps if you are wearing shoes with flexible soles that allow you to feel the ground. Place the side of your foot on the ground first, then roll your weight onto it slowly, keeping your balance with the other foot so you can pull back if you feel a twig underneath. Move slowly, taking just a step or two at a time before standing still for a minute or two to look and listen. If you make a noise accidentally, freeze in your tracks and wait until any creature alerted by the noise will have resumed what it was doing. The sound of the human voice is instantly recognised by all birds and animals, and you should avoid talking as much as possible. If you are chatting to a friend as you walk up to a wood, the damage will have been done, and it's too late keeping quiet once you are inside. If you are shooting with other people, agree on a series of hand signals so you can communicate in silence, and use a soft whistle to attract someone's attention rather than a shout of 'Hey, look!' or whatever.

Smell

Keen senses of sight and sound are common to all the airgun quarry species, but smell is only really a problem with the animals, particularly rabbits. A rabbit will scent you from several hundred yards away if the wind is blowing in the right direction, so you must work out which way the wind is blowing and plan your approach so that it carries your scent away from the quarry. The wind can play some funny tricks, blowing along valleys and round hills in a completely different direction, and it is difficult to allow for this unless you are familiar with the ground. In general, though, you are pretty safe if the wind is blowing directly from your quarry towards you, and this will also help to carry any sound you make away from your quarry. It can sometimes be difficult to tell which direction the wind is blowing if it is very light, so try dropping a few pieces of dry grass or fluff from your pockets and see which way they drift as they fall.

It may sometimes seem as though your quarry has a sixth sense, and can tell you are around despite all your efforts. Don't fool yourself, though. It can always be explained by one of your quarry's five senses – it's just that, being human, we aren't so aware of the noises, scents and sights around us.

For a successful stalk, you must first spot your quarry without alerting it to the fact you are there. This means moving very slowly around the shoot, flitting from one shadow to the next without making a sound. A good understanding of your quarry's habits and preferences will help enormously, because you will then know where to look and your chances of success will be greater. Never walk straight through a gate, or around the corner of a wood, otherwise you will show yourself to every creature for several hundred yards, and give yourself no chance of stalking it. Instead, edge round slowly, watching carefully for any signs of life: the tips of a rabbit's ears standing up above the grass, or the flash of sunlight on a pigeon's wing in a tree. A fox would stand for several minutes at the edge of the wood, watching for the tiniest movement – and so should you.

PLANNING THE STALK

Let's assume that you have spotted a rabbit which is feeding contentedly on the far side of the field. How are you going to go about putting it in the bag? The first part of any stalk is planning. Consider all the factors: which way the wind is blowing, how much cover there is between you and your quarry, and what its field of vision will be. Look at the lie of the land. Perhaps there is a hollow which will keep you hidden even though the grass is short. Are there any other creatures about which might sound a warning even though your quarry can't see you?

Once you have made your plan, be prepared to change it. You may find that your quarry has moved from its original position, and now has a better view, or a piece of cover that looked good from where you were standing may turn out to be too thin. More than once I have been caught out because the ground has been covered with dead leaves, or the husks of hazelnuts, and has been impossible to cross quietly.

Close to the quarry

As you approach closer to your quarry, you must move more slowly, and take even more care not to make a sound. To be sure of a clean kill, you will need to stalk within 20 to 25 yards, and at that distance the slightest noise will send the quarry scampering for safety. It is a good idea to cock and load your gun before you get too close, because it can be difficult to avoid making a noise doing this. With a spring air rifle, hold the trigger back as you cock the gun, and release it gently once the lever is in the rearward position. This avoids the click as the trigger sear engages in the piston notch. You can now bring the lever or barrel back to the closed position, being careful to avoid a click as the latch closes.

In the last few yards of the stalk, keep as close to the ground as possible, and keep your gun ahead of you and pointing towards the quarry. This is partly for safety reasons, but also the quarry sees less of the gun if it is pointing towards it. Watch the

Using a ditch as cover to approach the quarry.

quarry all the time as you stalk, and freeze if it raises its head. This means it has noticed something, and is looking and listening for signs of danger. You may even see a rabbit lift its nose and sniff the air. Wait until it lowers its head and resumes feeding before you move again.

You must be careful that your final shooting position does not leave any twigs or stalks in front of the muzzle, because even a tiny twig will deflect the pellet and cause a miss. I remember once stalking to within 15 yards of a rabbit, carefully lining up the cross-hairs and squeezing the trigger, thinking, 'That one's in the bag' – only to see the rabbit hop away through the scope. I raised my head in disbelief, and watched a large stinging nettle two yards away slowly topple and fall to the ground, with a neat pellet hole through its stem!

Remember that although the muzzle should be clear of obstructions, you must remain under cover or your quarry will spot you. Edge forward far enough for the muzzle to go just beyond the cover, but don't worry if there are stems and leaves in front of the scope. They won't stop you aiming, and they will help you to remain undetected.

Buck fever

At the end of a long stalk, you may find that you are unable to hold the gun steady. This is known as 'buck fever', and it's caused by the adrenalin pumping through your blood at the excitement and exertion of the stalk. Don't try to fight it, because the harder you try the more the gun will shake. Instead, relax and try to concentrate on breathing deeply and evenly. After a minute or so, raise the gun and try again. If you can force yourself to relax enough, you will overcome the problem – but it is something which affects even the most experienced hunter now and again.

Finally, after you have fired, don't jump up to collect your kill. Lie still for a minute or two in case there is any other quarry nearby. The sound of a shot will make them alert, but they may be confused and not know what to do. If you quietly cock the gun again and wait a few seconds, you may be rewarded with a second chance.

21. Shooting from a hide

There are times when stalking is the wrong approach – perhaps because you are trying to shoot a very wary bird such as a crow, or your quarry is hidden from view much of the time, as is the case with rabbits in the early summer when the crops and undergrowth are high.

In these situations, the alternative is to build a hide and lie in wait for your quarry to come to you. This has the advantage that you dictate the terms. You can select a spot that gives you a clear view of the target while remaining completely hidden. You don't need to move, so there is less chance of making a noise, and you avoid having to crawl through nettles, thistles and brambles. You can even build a seat so you can wait in comfort.

Hide shooting certainly has a lot going for it, but there's one big problem: there is no guarantee that the quarry will show up. This is where the real skill comes in. You must select the right place for the hide so that you stand the best chance of the quarry coming along, and wherever possible use decoys and calls to improve your chances.

The most obvious place to site a hide is at your quarry's feeding ground. To do this, you must know your quarry's feeding habits, and you would do well to spend several days beforehand simply watching and planning. Water can be a big attraction to birds and animals, too – especially during hot weather – so a pond or water trough may also be a good site for a hide. There is a lot of truth in the saying, 'Time spent in reconnaissance is seldom wasted'. If your recce shows you that the quarry is not feeding in a certain place, then that is valuable information, and the time has been well spent.

SITING THE HIDE

Once you have discovered where your quarry is feeding, and what times of the day are best, then you can begin to select the right spot for the hide. It should be within easy range of the feeding place, because there is no point in making things difficult for yourself. You need to bear in mind the direction of the wind, and watch the weather forecast to see whether a change is likely. Site the hide downwind, not just from the feeding place, but also the route that your quarry will take to get there. Plan to use natural cover as much as possible. Even the most realistic looking hide will stand out if it suddenly springs up overnight. As with stalking, you must be prepared to change your plans if necessary. The quarry may change its feeding habits for no apparent reason, for instance, or it may take a different route. On the day, the wind may be blowing from an unusual direction, or the farmer may have cut down the cover you had intended to use. You should always be ready to discard your original plans and think again.

Keep an open mind when you are siting a hide. Some of the most unlikely places can make excellent hides. I once had a very successful day's rabbit shooting from the driver's seat of an abandoned Morris Minor. The old car was facing a bank riddled with rabbit holes, and the windscreen had long since broken so that only a few pieces of shattered glass remained around the edges. The car had become a part of the scenery, and the rabbits ignored it. The only problem was that the springs had burst through the padding on the seat, which made it a little uncomfortable!

Hides do not always have to be at ground level. Deer stalkers often build 'high seats', which are in effect a hide on poles. Animals tend to look at ground level for danger, although rabbits also scan the sky for birds of prey. Another advantage of a hide above ground level is that your scent will blow over the top of your quarry, so it is less likely to detect you that way. For deer hunting with a powerful cartridge rifle, a high seat ensures that the bullet goes harmlessly into the ground, since you are firing downwards at the target. This is not usually a problem with an airgun, but in certain circumstances a hide in a tree could be your only safe option.

BUILDING THE HIDE

Every hide is different, depending on the type of cover available, the quarry you are hunting, and a host of other factors. There are some basic rules to follow, however. First, you should make use of natural cover as much as possible. The ideal hide is completely natural, and if you had time you would plant trees and bushes in exactly the right places. In real life this is not possible, but even when you are using camouflage netting you should make use of any natural cover available, and take branches from nearby trees to weave into the material.

Many shooters fall into the trap of building a box-shaped hide with poles and camouflage netting. This is not a natural shape,

A hide built in a tree provides a good vantage point to observe wildlife without disturbing it.

however, and inevitably stands out from the trees and bushes around. Remember that camouflage netting is not a natural material, and it always looks different from real foliage. You should treat camouflage netting as something that needs to be hidden, keeping it well back from the edge of a wood or hedge so that the sun does not shine directly on it. As part of your planning, you should select a spot where the sun will not move round so that it lights up you and your hide, because direct sunlight will see through even the best camouflage.

A hide should also be as light and portable as possible. You may need to move from one place to another if your quarry's feeding habits change during the day, or if your shooting disturbs them so they move elsewhere. For this reason, I prefer the modern plastic netting, which doesn't absorb water like the old-fashioned hessian type. After a shower of rain, the old netting used to become very heavy to carry, and took several days to dry out again.

You can easily get carried away building a large, elaborate hide that is like a home from home. But it's far more effective to keep the hide very small. Don't use the full area of your camouflage netting just because it's there. Use as much as you need and no more, bunching the rest up on the floor of the hide if necessary, or even doubling it over to give a second layer of netting.

When I set off for a day's hide shooting, I carry very little equipment over and above what I would take for stalking. A game bag containing a knife, a length of string and a small section of camouflage netting is all you need. Poles are unncessary, because you can always find something which will support the camouflage netting, even if it is just a bramble stalk. Choose your spot, then set up your netting from behind the cover rather than in front of it. You want to hide the camouflage netting behind the bushes, not the other way around. Using as little netting as possible, make sure that your entire body is hidden from view, not just from the front but also the sides – and the top, too, if you are shooting birds such as crows or pigeons. Shotgunners need not worry about being seen from

Weaving natural vegetation into a net to make a hide.

above, because they can shoot birds on the wing, but with an airgun you must allow the birds to settle undisturbed before you can shoot. Remember that you will have to shoot through the camouflage netting rather than over it, otherwise your quarry will spot you peering over the top of the hide. Follow the natural shapes of the bushes when you set up the netting, and avoid creating any straight lines, either horizontally or vertically.

Once the camouflage netting is set up, sit in the hide and check whether there are any stems in your field of fire. Cut these down with the knife, and weave them into the netting, taking care to put them the right way up. Most leaves are lighter in colour on the underside, and will look suspicious if you put them in upside-down. Once the hide is finished, take a few steps back and examine it carefully. If you have done the job properly, you should find it difficult to see where the hide is; if you can spot it too easily, perhaps you should think again.

USING DECOYS

Setting up pigeon decoys for a day's hide shooting.

This is the time to set up any decoys that you plan to use. For pigeons, you need to build up a decoy 'pattern' that looks like a flock of birds feeding, and the more decoys you use the better. Remember to set them facing more or less into the wind, so that they look realistic. Pigeons joining a flock will come in into the wind, and drop into the rearmost part of the pattern, so bear

this in mind when you site the 'deeks'. There are many different types of pigeon decoy, but my favourites are the 'shell' type which are made of very thin plastic moulded into a hollow pigeon shape. They are very light to carry, and they 'nest' into one another, so you can easily carry a couple of dozen in a game bag. You will need to use the special pegs to hold them in position, because they are so light the slightest breeze will blow them away. If you set them up properly on the pegs, they will rock back and forth in the wind, giving a realistic feeding movement.

The shell type of pigeon decoy is very light and easy to carry, but once set up on its special peg it provides a realistic effect.

For crows, magpies and jays, an owl decoy can sometimes be effective, especially if you combine it with a good decoy call. Calls are not easy to use, and you would be well advised to practise before trying it for real – but they can work very well in the right circumstances.

Other quarry, such as rabbits and squirrels, do not take any notice of decoys, so you simply have to watch and wait.

WAITING IN THE HIDE

Waiting in a hide can be very tedious, with nothing to do for hours on end. You must learn to be patient if you are going to succeed. Even when you cannot see your quarry, you must keep still and silent. There may be a rabbit warily sniffing the air outside its burrow at precisely the moment you decide to stretch your legs. Hearing you move about will send it back under-ground for another hour or two – or all day if you quarry has been hunted regularly.

While you are waiting, keep a careful eye out for any sign of your quarry feeding elsewhere. Pigeons are notorious for changing their feeding places and flight-lines for no apparent reason, and you may notice a new flight-line developing which shows you they have moved on to another field. If so, don't waste good shooting time by sitting in a duff spot. Dismantle your hide as quickly as possible and move to where the birds are. There may even be days when shooting from a hide turns out to be a dead loss, and you might as well try stalking instead.

TAKING THE SHOT

Taking a shot from a hide is a lot easier than after a stalk. You are naturally more relaxed, and your body does not have to cope with the exertion of crawling through the undergrowth. You can select a good shooting position well in advance, and you are less likely to suffer from 'buck fever'. Don't rush to take the shot. If you have built the hide properly, your quarry will be off guard, and you will have plenty of time to settle yourself into the right position for a steady shot. More often than not, your quarry will not appear just where you expected, and you will have to adjust your angle to shoot. Do so slowly to avoid alarming it: a couple of seconds of hurried movement at this point will waste hours of patient waiting. A shotgunner can afford to pop up and shoot his quarry as it flees, but with an airgun you must remain hidden until the moment the pellet strikes.

A hide should be kept as small as possible, and should include vegetation collected from nearby.

Slide the muzzle gently through the camouflage so you can be sure the pellet won't catch on the netting on its way to the target. Everything else needs to remain completely hidden behind the camouflage, of course, so don't be tempted to push the scope through for a clearer view.

As with stalking, always remember that there may be other quarry around which could be confused by your shot, and may give you the chance of a second kill. Indeed, unless your first kill is lying where it will frighten others away, it is often best to leave it where it falls, and only collect it when it is time to go home. The sound of an airgun firing will only disturb creatures a hundred yards or so away, but the sight of you setting off to collect your kill will alarm anything within half a mile or more.

22. Around the farm buildings

There are various types of vermin that you are most likely to shoot not in the fields and woods, but among the farm buildings, perhaps only a few yards from the farmhouse doorstep. The techniques you need to use are a combination of stalking and hide shooting, with a few special tactics thrown in as well.

The main quarry that you will be hunting around the farmyard is rats and collared doves. On rare occasions, you may have to deal with other pests, such as grey squirrels for instance, but rats and collared doves are usually the biggest problem around farm buildings because they soon become used to the comings and goings of people and machinery and will make their home close to the grain and feed stores which provide them with easy pickings. The amount of food that they actually eat is not all that great, but the damage they do can be serious. Rats will gnaw through the structure of the buildings, as well as pipes and cables, while both rats and collared doves foul grain and feed with their droppings, spoiling much more than they eat.

Although rats and collared doves around farm buildings soon become used to people working nearby, they seem to know when they are in danger. This is because people behave differently when they are shooting. A farm worker will walk purposefully across the yard and into a building without hesitating, even if he notices the collared doves sitting on the roof above. A shooter, on the other hand, creeps around slowly, stopping and looking about him all the time. If he spots a collared dove on the roof of a building, he stops in his tracks, and turns towards it. No wonder his quarry feels threatened!

When shooting around the farmyard you must do the same as when stalking a wary rabbit in a field and keep out of sight right up to the moment you fire. It's no good thinking that it will be easy because your quarry is used to seeing people around. Fortunately, the farmyard is full of cover that you can hide behind. There are the buildings themselves, plus all the different bits of machinery that you find around the farm.

You need to remember that a farmyard can be a very dangerous place. Many people each year are killed and injured by farm machinery, and if you are not familiar with the equipment you are even more at risk. Many pieces of farm machinery can be switched on from a distance, such as the augers used to move grain from one place to another. A farm worker could switch on an auger without realising that you have your foot on the other end – with horrifying results. Treat farm animals with respect, too. Most people would have the sense to keep away from a bull, but even cows can be dangerous if they are frightened, and pigs can inflict a nasty bite. The best advice is to keep out of any enclosure with livestock in it. Don't assume that you can out-run a farm animal. They can move surprisingly quickly, and there is always the chance you could slip up. You must also be aware that the farm work must go on – it cannot stop just because you are shooting. Don't get in the way of tractors and other equipment, and always ask beforehand where you can and cannot go.

For the same reasons, you must also be very careful about where you shoot. Always assume that there might be a farm worker around the next corner, or in a building, and don't shoot if you can't be sure of where the pellet will go.

COLLARED DOVES

The best way to shoot collared doves is usually to find their favourite resting places and hide up where you can get a clear shot at them. Collared doves will normally have a favourite roof where they like to sit to see that the coast is clear before they swoop down to feed. A little observation will soon show you their favourite places, and you can then find a suitable place to hide. This might be behind a pile of straw bales, inside a building, or even in the cab of a tractor that is not being used.

Follow the same rules as you would for hide shooting in the field. Find a spot where you are in the shade, and keep well back under cover. People often forget the basic principles when they are shooting from buildings. Don't stand right beside the window, and poke the gun outside. You will be plainly visible from outside. Instead, stay well back inside the building, where any light coming in will not reach you.

Once you have selected a good spot, you can then settle down and wait for your quarry to come back. As with any form of hide shooting, you will have to be patient, but with collared doves you usually don't have so long to wait. Collared doves may be more tame than their cousins out in the fields, but they are not stupid and they will soon learn to be wary if they are shot at a few times. Try to avoid shooting when there are several of the birds about. It's best to shoot individual birds, rather than waiting until there are several sitting together. That way, they don't get the chance to learn about the danger.

Many farm buildings have quite fragile roofs and gutters, which can easily be damaged by a powerful air rifle. The farmer won't be pleased if you shoot a hole in the roof of his barn, no matter how many collared doves you have killed, so take care. It's also a good idea to remove the bodies of any birds you have shot, even if they lodge in the gutter or on the roof. A carcase will block the gutter, and cause the water to cascade down the side of the building next time it rains, and once again this won't improve your chances of being asked back to shoot another time. You must be extremely careful about climbing onto the roof, though, because it is unlikely to support your weight. If the bird is out of reach, use a long pole or stick to drag it close enough to reach without getting onto the roof. If in doubt, tell the farmer what has happened, and ask him whether he would like you to retrieve your kill.

RATS

Rats require a different approach. You can shoot them success- fully by hiding close to their feeding places, but the best bet is usually to stalk them around the yard and buildings at dusk. Collared doves generally congregate together in one spot, whereas rats will have many different holes around the farmyard, and may only go a few feet from the entrance to feed. By shooting from a hide, you will only see a fraction of the rats in the area, unless there is one feeding place that they all come to, such as a grain store.

Rats tend to come out to feed as night falls, so you will need a good scope and some sort of artifical light to shoot them effectively. The experts say that rats' eyes are less sensitive to red light, so you might like to fit a red filter over any light you use. Personally, I have found that an ordinary white light is fine so long as it is not too bright. A powerful torch fitted on your gun is very useful, or if you are shooting inside buildings you can leave a light on. If you plan to leave the lights on for shooting, it's a good idea to leave them burning for several nights before you intend to shoot, so the rats can become used to feeding in the light. Your first couple of shots will scare them away, so the best tactic is to move from one building to the next, trying to shoot a couple of rats in each place before leaving them to settle down again. As with any form of shooting in and around buildings, you must be extra careful not to cause any damage with your pellets. This is where an airgun really scores over a shotgun or cartridge rifle, because it is far less likely to damage the building.

I once spent a very exciting night with a friend shooting rats on a chicken farm. The hens were kept in sheds full of battery cages, with a thousand or more in each shed. There were six or seven sheds, plus other buildings such as feed stores and grain bins. This meant that we could move from one building to the next, and by the time we got back to the first one again the rats had had enough time to regain their confidence and come back out to feed.

We left a dim light burning in each shed, just enough to shoot by without alarming the rats. We would sneak into a shed, and the two of us would each pick a target. On the count of three, we would both fire at the same time. With luck, that meant two rats dead. Then all hell would break loose, as the other rats scampered for safety. There were rats everywhere, on top of and even inside the battery cages, where they ate the chickens' food and any eggs they had laid. If a chicken died during the night, there would be nothing but bones left in the morning. We would reload as quickly as possible and try to shoot the rats as they dived for cover, but there was little chance of hitting the fleeing shapes. Occasionally one would stop at the entrance to its hole, giving us the chance of a stationary shot. I will never forget my amazement at how many rats there were in such a small space. The whole floor seemed to come alive, and the rats would rush headlong against our wellingtons in their hurry to escape. It was glad I had remembered to tuck my trousers into my boots, in case a rat saw my trouser leg as a handy bolt-hole! I lost count of how many rats we killed that night, but there seemed to be corpses everywhere, although it made little difference to the number of rats we saw running around. In the morning, there wasn't a dead rat in sight. I don't know whether it was the farm cats or the rats themselves, but something had moved every single body.

There is a lot of superstition surrounding rats, and every countryman will have weird tales to tell about encounters with the creatures. You need to treat rats with respect, because they carry disease and will bite if cornered, but many of these stories are wildly exaggerated. There is something about rats that sets the imagination going, especially when you are alone at night, and more than once I have lost my nerve when rat shooting and run out of a building in blind panic. Perhaps this is why people make up stories about rats as big as dogs – they don't like to admit they were scared of something no bigger than their shoe!

23. Handling and preparing game

Many of the typical airgun quarry are delicious to eat, but you need to know how to handle and prepare them properly so that they reach the table in the best condition. In fact, virtually any animal or bird can be eaten, but you would have to be on the verge of starvation to want to eat a rat! Rabbits and pigeons make very good eating, and some people also like eating squirrel – in the States, squirrel is considered quite a delicacy, and I am told it tastes like chicken, although I have never tried it myself.

Looking after game for the pot starts even before you pull the trigger. When you're shooting a pigeon or rabbit to eat, you should consider not just how to achieve a clean kill, but also how to avoid spoiling the meat. This tends to be more important with a shotgun, which can make a terrible mess of the quarry if you shoot it at close range. But even with an airgun, you should try to avoid hitting the parts of your quarry which have the best meat.

DISPATCHING GAME

Occasionally you may find that your quarry is not killed cleanly, and you must then finish it off as quickly as possible so that it doesn't suffer. The quickest way is to fire another pellet into its head at short range. If this isn't possible, perhaps because you have left your gun back in your hide, you can kill a bird or animal very quickly and painlessly with your hands. With a bird, you must wring its neck. Hold its body in one hand, and take the head in the other hand. Twist the head round one half turn, then reposition your hand so you can give it another quick full turn, pulling at the same time. Keep twisting until you feel the neck break and the bird go limp. Done properly, this is all over in under a second, and the bird does not suffer.

With a rabbit, you must again break its neck, but you do this in a different way. Hold the rabbit by its back legs in one hand, and take the head in your other hand, with the neck in the gap between your thumb and forefinger. Then pull your hands firmly apart, twisting your hand so as to pull the rabbit's head up and back. Once again, you will feel the creature's neck break, and it will go limp.

These techniques are very effective when carried out properly, and cause the creature no suffering. You would be well advised to practise on dead birds and animals first, so you know what to do when you are faced with dispatching a live creature for the first time.

AFTER THE KILL

When you have shot your quarry, pick it up as soon as possible, rather than leaving it where flies or even a fox can get at it. If it's a rabbit, you should empty its bladder so that it can't leak at the wrong moment. To do this, hold the rabbit upside-down by its front legs, and run your thumb firmly along its belly towards the back legs. Next, check its ears for fleas. Most rabbits have plenty of fleas around their ears, and you don't want to take them home with you as well. If you are staying out in the field for a while, you should then hang it in a cool, shady place where it will be out of reach of foxes and cats. Don't stuff it into a game bag where it will get overheated and squashed. At home, if you are not going to deal with it straight away, find a cool place free from flies to hang your game. If you shoot game often, you may decide to build a special game larder. This can be an old wardrobe or cupboard out of doors away from direct sunlight. Make holes to allow the air to circulate, and cover these with a fine mesh to keep flies out. Make sure that the doors fit tightly, because flies will squeeze through the smallest hole if they know there is food around. Remember that game will drip blood and goodness knows what else when you hang it up, so don't hang it over anything that might be damaged or difficult to clean. You won't be very popular if you hang it in the garage over the car, for instance!

Some types of game are improved by hanging for a few days. This is normally done with pheasants and grouse, for instance. The idea is that the meat starts to break down, making it more tender and tastier. Airgun quarry should normally be prepared and cooked as soon as possible after being shot, however, since hanging will not improve them.

PREPARING A PIGEON

Birds need to be plucked before cooking. This job is best done out of doors, or at least in the shed, because the feathers get everywhere. Hold the bird in your left hand, lying on its back with the head away from you. With your right hand, take a few feathers between finger and thumb, and pull them out with a sharp tug away from you. Work over a cardboard box or dustbin so the feathers go straight into the bin instead of blowing about. Slowly work your way around the bird, pulling all the feathers off its body, legs and neck. A pheasant's feathers are very firmly attached, but pigeons pluck quite easily, and you will soon be able to pluck these birds in next to no time. The BASC run a pigeon plucking competition at the Game Fair, and the winners can pluck a bird in under a minute. Once the bird is plucked, you must remove the feet, wings and head. The wings can be chopped off close to the body with a heavy knife or strong pair of scissors, but leave sufficient skin so that it does not shrink back and expose the breast meat when you cook it. For the same reason, you should cut the neck quite close to the head, then roll the skin back and cut through the neckbone close to the body – leaving a generous flap of skin to help cover the breast. The legs should be bent back to snap the knuckle joint, then pull the feet off rather than cut them so you withdraw the strong sinews that work the toes.

Next, you must remove the innards. To do this, lay the bird on its back and make a vertical cut at the anus, large enough for you to insert two fingers. Push your fingers in as far as they will go, and hook them around the stomach and intestines. Holding the bird over a bin or an old newspaper, pull out the intestines, making sure you have left nothing behind. You may need to go in from the neck end to make sure of removing the heart and lungs. Then rinse the bird under the tap, and it's ready for cooking.

To save all this trouble, some people take the easy way out with pigeons, and simply cut off the meat on either side of the breast with a sharp knife. Lay the bird on its back, separate the feathers down the middle of the breast, and cut the skin along the line of the breastbone. You can now peel the skin back, revealing the breast meat which can be cut away from the bone in the same way as you would fillet a fish. The rest of the bird, which contains very little meat anyway, can be thrown away. Whether you use this method or pluck the bird in the normal way depends on how you plan to cook it. Pigeons can be roasted like a chicken, in which case you should allow one bird per person. Personally, I find the meat rather dry and tough cooked this way, and I prefer pigeon cooked in a casserole, with vegetables and perhaps some other meat as well.

PREPARING A RABBIT

To prepare a rabbit for the pot, you need to skin it, remove the innards, feet, tail and head, and then cut it into smaller pieces or joints. The skin of a rabbit comes off quite easily, but you need to go about removing it the right way to avoid spoiling the meat. If you want to keep the skin, perhaps to line a jacket, then you must be extra careful because it tears very easily.

Start by collecting together everything you will need: plenty of old newspaper, knives of different sizes, a chopping board, and a plate or dish for the joints of meat. Lay the rabbit on its back, and pinch the skin on its belly between your finger and thumb. You can then make a cut into the skin without pushing the knife through the stomach wall into the intestines. You should try to carry out the entire operation without breaking the intestines, because the contents are most unpleasant! Once again, an airgun scores over a shotgun, because a rabbit killed by a shotgun will usually have dozens of punctures in the intestine where the pellets struck.

Extend the first cut up towards the rabbit's head, and down between the back legs, using the knife upside-down and cutting upwards. You can then peel the skin away from the flesh beneath, turning the skin inside-out as though you were removing a well-fitting overall. The skin will be attached firmly at the feet, tail and neck, so you need to chop these off to remove the skin entirely. If you plan to use the skin, cut up the inside of each leg so as to open up the skin completely, otherwise the skin will go bad inside the leg-holes. You will

Skinning a rabbit – the dog wanted to help!

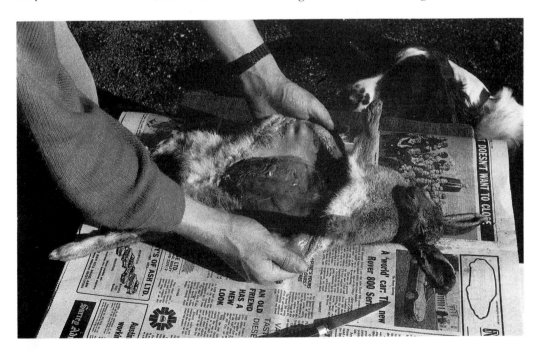

need to cut through the bones at the legs and neck, which will require a hefty chop on the board with a stout knife – mind your fingers!

The next step is to remove the intestines. If you have done the first part properly, you will now have to slit the muscle wall surrounding the innards. Make a cut along the length of the rabbit's belly, just as you did with the skin, using the knife upside-down once again. The cut should stretch from between the back legs up to the bottom of the rib cage. Fold back the flaps of skin and, holding the rabbit upright over a bin or newspaper, hook your fingers round the stomach. Pull out the stomach, and the intestines should follow. Make sure you have removed all the intestines, and lay the rabbit down again. You should find the liver and kidneys still in position. Remove these, and save them for cooking, but check the liver first for signs of disease. Many rabbits have diseased livers, and although I don't think this could be passed on by eating it after cooking, I for one wouldn't like to try.

You can now trim away the flaps of skin that held the intestines in place. These are no good for eating, so throw them away. Push your finger into the pelvic cavity to dislodge any faeces that might remain there. You must now remove the lungs and heart, which are hidden behind the diaphragm inside the rib cage. Push your fingers through the diaphragm and pull it away to reveal the lungs and heart, which you can then hook out with your finger. Some people keep these to eat, but I don't like them so I throw them away or give them to the dog. After a quick rinse under the tap, you should be left with nothing but good, clean meat, and all that remains is to cut it into joints for cooking.

Start by removing the legs. The front legs have no bones attaching them to the body, so you can slip your knife between the shoulder blade and the rib cage, gently easing the leg away from the body. The back legs are attached by a ball and socket joint at the hip, and you will need to dislocate the joint by bending the leg backwards before cutting the leg away from the body. The rib cage has very little meat on it, and I usually prefer to trim the ribs off with a strong pair of scissors. Then cut the meat along the backbone into good sized saddle portions. For this you will need a heavy knife or meat cleaver, because you must break through the backbone which is surprisingly strong. You now have seven or eight good joints of meat which are delicious in a casserole or pie.

CURING A SKIN

I rarely bother to keep a rabbit's skin, but they can be used for a variety of purposes. In days gone by, the fur was used to make felt hats, and you can join a number of skins together to make clothing – although it's hardly the sort of thing you would wear to work, or to the disco! Rabbit skins could make a warm lining for a jacket, however. Another use for them is to cover a dummy for training a dog to retrieve game.

To cure a skin, you must stretch it out to dry, because any moisture in the skin will cause it to rot. Make sure that you have opened it out completely by cutting up the insides of the legs and neck. Then stretch it out on a board, pinning it down all round the edge with tacks. Use a sharp knife to scrape off any remaining flesh or fat, then rub in crystals of alum, which you can buy from a chemist. The alum must be rubbed in thoroughly, then leave the skin in a warm, dry place where the air can circulate freely around it but where it is safe from flies. Go back to it every few days and rub in a bit more alum. It may take several weeks for the skin to dry out thoroughly, but be patient. If you don't let it dry properly, it will soon rot.

Once the skin is dry, you can use it for whatever purpose you have in mind. It will be very stiff, though, so you may need to rub in some boot dubbin (on the non-furry side!) to make it more pliable. You will find it quite easy to sew, but a rabbit's skin is only thin and has little strength, so don't expect too much of it. It is best used as a lining rather than as the basis of a piece of clothing itself.

24. Somewhere to shoot

One of the biggest problems faced by many newcomers to airgun hunting is finding somewhere to shoot. There are a few lucky people who live on a farm, or who have access to a shoot through a friend, but for the majority of people who take up airgun hunting, finding a shoot can be hard, frustrating work.

There are no hard and fast rules on how to go about it, and you may try for ages only to come across somewhere from the most unlikely source. One thing is certain, though. You won't find a shoot by sitting at home – you have to go out and look for it.

The first thing is to keep your ears and eyes open. Put the word about that you are looking for a place to shoot, and listen for any chance remark which might be worth following up. You might hear someone in a pub complaining about the damage the rabbits are doing on his land, for instance. That's your cue to sympathise with him – and then suggest that you could help him out.

As you travel around, watch for signs of vermin causing damage, which might give you a chance to find the farmer and offer to control them. You might spot a flock of woodpigeons feeding on an unprotected crop of oilseed rape, for example, or a large number·of rabbits feeding on a particular field. Then you can knock on the farmer's door, say that you were passing and noticed the problem, and wondered if you could help. With luck, he will be impressed that you have noticed his predicament, and will be more inclined to give you a chance to prove your worth.

Failing this, you can even go knocking on doors, to ask whether the farmer has a vermin problem that you could help to control. Get hold of a copy of the Ordnance Survey map for your area, and draw a circle around your home which shows the distance you can reasonably travel. Then mark all the farms in that area, and systematically go round each and every one. You will find that there are good and bad times of the day to catch farmers at home. Usually they will be out in the fields from early in the morning, and return to the farmhouse for lunch. That may be a good time to call, or perhaps later in the day after they have returned for the evening – although if it's a busy time of year such as harvest time they will be out virtually twenty-four hours a day and have other things on their mind.

APPROACHING A FARMER

It's important to create the right impression when you go calling on farmers, whether you know they have a vermin problem or not. Put yourself in the farmer's shoes. There he is, enjoying a well-earned rest in front of the telly, when there is a knock on the door. It's someone he has never seen in his life before, asking permission to wander around his land with a gun. Naturally enough, he will be cautious – just as you would if someone asked to shoot in your back garden. First impressions will make all the difference. If you are dressed like Rambo, with full camouflage, a huge knife on your belt, and a rifle under your arm, he won't be too happy about letting you loose on his farm. Dress smartly, and leave your gun and camouflage at home – or at least in the car. Show him that you know about the countryside, by talking knowledgeably about farming and the pests that need to be controlled. Tell him that you are a member of the BASC (there's another good reason to join if you haven't already). Explain that you will respect his crops and livestock, keep within the boundaries that he sets you, and you won't shoot the game birds. You are trying to build up a picture of someone who is responsible and will cause no problems for the farmer, but will help him by controlling the vermin.

Even if you do everything right, there may be perfectly good reasons why he can't let you shoot on his farm. Perhaps he has already given permission to someone else, or the shooting rights are let to a game shooting syndicate who also control the vermin. If he says no, accept it gracefully and try elsewhere. Unless you are very lucky, you will be turned away many times before you find someone who will listen. Perseverance is the name of the game, so don't be discouraged. Remember too that there are many places other than farms which may be suffering from vermin. A local water works, golf course or power station may have problems with rabbits, for instance, while many large buildings suffer from too many feral pigeons. I have had good sport in some unlikely places – such as the grounds of a nursing home and even my own school's playing fields which were being damaged by rabbits – although I was only allowed to shoot there in the holidays.

GOING BEATING

Even if you cannot find somewhere straight away, there are things you can do to get closer to the people who hold the power to grant you shooting rights. The better they get to know you, and realise that you are a responsible person, the better your chances. Most game shoots need beaters during the shooting season, to help drive the birds out of cover and over the guns. Find out where your local game shoots are, and contact the gamekeeper to ask him whether he needs beaters. As a beater, you have the chance to get to know the keeper himself, as well as the other beaters – all of whom may know someone who knows someone who has somewhere you could shoot. This sort of personal contact is probably the best way to find shooting. Beating is actually great fun in its own right. You spend a day in the countryside, in the company of people with similar interests to your own – and you get paid for it as well. Remember that you are being watched all the time, and the keeper and others will soon notice if you stray out of line or spend all your time chatting rather than getting on with the job – and that won't improve your chances one bit.

JOIN A CLUB

Another way to find shooting is to join a club. There are many vermin control clubs around the country, most of which are affiliated to the BASC. These clubs offer their services to local farmers, and can often stand a better chance of gaining his approval than an individual shooter would. The farmer feels that he can trust a club to check out its members thoroughly, and make sure that they behave responsibly. These clubs usually consist mainly of shotgunners, but they would be happy to consider an airgunner for membership. Even a field target airgun club may provide you with a contact who can suggest somewhere you could shoot, and being a member of any club adds an air of respectability when you go knocking on farmhouse doors.

PAYING FOR SHOOTING

If all else fails, you may consider paying for the privilege of shooting. That may not sound too attractive, but it's what game shooters have to do – and with more and more people wanting to shoot on the same amount of land, it's the way things are going. Shooting rights can be expensive, so the best bet is probably to club together with some friends and see how much you can afford by pooling your resources. After all, you are likely to end up with more shooting than one person could cope with on his own. You might even decide to set up a formal club if there isn't one already in your area. Subscriptions could go into a fund to pay for a shoot, and you might find that one or two of your members had ideas where you could try. If not, you could advertise in a farming paper such as *Farmers Weekly*, or write to local farmers on behalf of the club.

Like most things in life that are worth having, shooting doesn't always come easily, but that's all the more reason to keep trying.

BEHAVIOUR ON THE SHOOT

Once you have found somewhere to shoot, you will want to keep it – and that means not doing anything to upset the farmer or gamekeeper. Remember that it is not just you who is judged by your actions, but all airgunners. If you behave badly and get thrown off the shoot, the farmer will be in no hurry to let another airgunner use his land.

Start by listening to the farmer, and taking note of what you can and cannot do. There may be certain fields or woods that you should keep out of, for instance, and he will also tell you where the boundaries of his land are. He may want certain quarry species left alone, or he may ask you to concentrate on a particular vermin problem rather than just wander about aimlessly. Respect his wishes, because he will soon find out if you are straying out of bounds or shooting forbidden quarry – and you will be sent packing. It is important to show the farmer that you are actually doing some good by controlling the vermin that is troubling him. He won't be very impressed if the pigeons continue to destroy his crop of rape despite your efforts. Take the trouble to call at the farm after you have finished shooting, and tell him what you have shot. It doesn't matter if you haven't made a big bag. He will be happy to know that you have been around, helping to scare the birds away.

For the same reason, you should make yourself available if he calls you up to deal with a particular problem. Perhaps a newly drilled crop of wheat is taking a hammering from the pigeons. He won't be too pleased if you say you can't come this weekend because you have made other plans. You can get away with it once or twice, but sooner or later the farmer will find someone else who can do a better job of protecting his crops.

And after you've gone to such trouble to find a shoot, the last thing you want is to lose it and have to start looking all over again.

Section III

FIELD TARGET
SHOOTING

25. The field target scene

Field target shooting is a relatively new sport. It has only been in existence for a few years, and I remember not so long ago helping out at some of the *Airgun World* championships which really started the ball rolling. The sport may be young, but it has come on in leaps and bounds in a few short years. There are now over two hundred clubs up and down the country catering specially for field target enthusiasts, each organising their own competitions and many of them entering teams for national events. Individual shooters travel miles to compete in major events such as the championships supported by the leading airgun magazines. The sport has even begun to attract sponsorship from outside the airgun industry itself, with sponsors such as the Anglia Building Society.

It is an encouraging start for a great sport, but field target shooting has now reached an important crossroads. It has grown to the point where there is now a desperate need for a strong governing body to set standards and lay down rules, to ensure the highest standard of sportsmanship and safety, and so that everyone knows where they stand. But for the moment, let's look at exactly what field target shooting is all about, and why it has such an enormous appeal to different types of shooters.

One of the great attractions of field target shooting, to my mind, is that it is done outdoors, in conditions close to those you would encounter when hunting. If it is raining, or blowing a gale, that's too bad. You must shoot to the best of your ability in the conditions prevailing on the day and this adds an extra dimension to the sport which wouldn't be there if you shot indoors.

THE TARGETS

The targets are designed to look like real airgun quarry – squirrels, rats, rabbits, crows and so on. They consist of a flat metal plate cut to the shape of the quarry, with a 45mm (1¾-inch) hole or 'kill zone' cut out of it. Behind this hole is a striker plate, which allows the target to fall over if your pellet passes through the hole and hits it. If you hit the silhouette but miss the hole, the target remains upright and you score a miss. The target can be reset from the firing point by pulling a string, which saves you having to walk up and down to reset after each hit. Some of the first field targets were unreliable, and led to many arguments over whether or not the shooter had hit the kill zone. Nowadays, field targets have been improved so that there is no argument. The most popular target is the Knokdown, made by the Welham family who are familiar faces on the field target circuit, but others such as the Mede target are also used.

The Knok-Down target is used by many field target clubs.

THE COMPETITION

A field target competition course will consist of a number of targets set up along a course, with a firing point marked out for each target. You start at firing point 1 and fire one shot at target number 1. The scorer records on your card whether you scored a hit or a miss, and you move on to firing point 2 to shoot at the second target. Meanwhile, the next shooter in line takes your place at the first firing point . . . and so on. To save time, firing points are often grouped together so you stay in one position to shoot at targets 5, 6 and 7, for instance. When you have completed the course, you hand your card to the official who keeps the scores, and the winner is the shooter who makes the highest score during the day. It's basically very simple, which is part of the attraction. But the organisers can make each target as difficult or as easy as they like. In any one competition, you are likely to find targets in all kinds of situations – near and far, up a tree, in a dip, behind an obstruction. Some targets have to be shot from the standing position, while for others you can use any position you like. All this means that no two shoots are the same. Every shooter has to deal with the same course of targets in a given competition, but you could enter a different competition every week of your life, and never see two exactly alike. That's another point in favour of field target shooting – you never get bored with shooting at the same targets in the same conditions. Just as in real hunting, you are always having to overcome new problems.

In fact, field target shooting brings together some of the best aspects of both hunting and target shooting. It has the thrill of competition, with the chance to meet and chat to people who share your interests. It encourages and rewards skill and dedication. And it takes you outside to pit your wits against the elements and the organisers who set up the targets. You must be skilled at judging range and wind, and able to shoot with great accuracy. You can take part at all levels, whether you are a

A 'dump-shoot' is a popular side event at many field target competitions.

novice or a dedicated expert shot. You can set out to win, or you can just go along for the atmosphere and a chance to fire your gun. Most field target shoots have other events running alongside the main competition. There is usually a plinking range where you can fire away to your heart's content at various targets. Often there will also be smaller competitions – such as a long-range target competition, a 'bird shoot' consisting of pigeon and crow targets, or a 'dump shoot' with rats and rabbits set out among piles of rubble and broken prams to look like a rubbish tip.

The plinking range at a field target shoot.

HOW THE SPORT IS ORGANISED

I mentioned earlier that field target shooting is at a crossroads. The reason is simply that it has become so successful, and it has grown beyond the stage where it can afford to be run in an informal way. Many of the bigger championships attract two hundred entrants or more, and all too often the numbers stretch the organisation to the limit – and beyond. You find shooters queuing for hours for their turn to shoot, unable to wander around and enjoy the other attractions of the day. A slow shooter holds up all those behind him, so queues build up at the firing points too. Shooters turn up late in the day and expect to be allowed to enter, so the prizegiving ceremony is pushed back later and later until after many people have gone home. Even with the excellent modern targets, there are sometimes problems over whether or not a target has been killed. And there are dark mutterings about so-and-so's gun being 'over the limit' where the organisers have decided not to bother with a chronograph test.

The informal approach is fine for a friendly competition at a local club, but when there are big prizes and titles at stake, competitiors have a right to expect the shoot to run like clockwork. The only way to achieve this, and avoid arguments, is to have a proper set of rules laid down by an official body which has the power to enforce them. The rules must be followed nationwide, so that every shoot from the club 'friendly' to a national championship is run in the same way. A shooter from Wales used to competing in his local inter-club matches could travel to a national championship in Scotland and know that he would be playing by the same rules, and clubs or individual shooters who broke the rules would be disqualified from entering other events for a fixed period of time.

Various organisations, such as NARPA, the National Air Rifle and Pistol Association, have looked as though they were going to take over the role of official governing body for field target shooting, only to fade away from the scene. The British Field Target Association has gone some way towards this ideal, but there is still plenty more work to be done. At present it depends entirely on the hard work put in by a few volunteers, who have to hold down full-time jobs as well. There are moves afoot to appoint a full-time BFTA official, which to my mind would be the best thing to happen to field target shooting for a long time. Only then can it really take the lead and show the sport the way forward. Without this, I feel that there is a real danger of the sport dying on its feet, as competitors become fed up with the lack of organisation and drift away to take up other sports. Field target shooters must not stand by and wait for someone to take the bull by the horns. It is up to the shooters themselves to set up the necessary framework, and then support it by keeping up their subscriptions to their local clubs. Only then can the sport cope with the number of followers that it deserves, and attract the kind of publicity and sponsorship needed for it to thrive. Who knows, we may yet see field target air rifle shooting become a major international sport.

There is much more development to come before the sport reaches that level of respectability, though. A chronograph test for every competitor is essential, in my opinion. At every shoot you will find a minority whose guns are nudging over the legal limit, and this simply causes ill-feeling among those who stick to the rules. A compulsory chronograph test for every gun, using a standard pellet and chronograph, would put a stop to all that, and ensure that everyone competes on the same terms.

The equipment used by some of the top competitors nowadays has become highly sophisticated, and newcomers and those who cannot afford the best gun and scope are handicapped from the start. I believe that there should be separate classes for different age groups and types of gun, to ensure that everyone has a chance of sharing in the prizes.

Proper organisation of shoots, with squadding and time limits for each firing point would control the sometimes horrendous queues which turn what should be an enjoyable day out into something about as exciting as waiting for a bus. The number of entries in any given shoot should be restricted to a fixed number, published in advance, so that everyone knows they must arrive in good time to be sure of a chance to enter. And the prizegiving ceremony should go ahead at the fixed time, come hell or high water.

Field target shooting has a great future ahead of it, but only if the shooters themselves get organised. Far from destroying the appeal of the sport, it will ensure that everyone can enjoy it, without the bitter arguments and frustration that all too often mar competitions today.

26. How to start

Let's suppose that you have decided you would like to try your hand at field target shooting. You have read about it in the airgun magazines, and think it could be the sport for you. Where do you start?

Field target shooting is, of course, something that you do with other people. Unlike in hunting, you can't have a field target shoot on your own. All right, so you could set up a field target in your back garden and shoot at it. You could even keep a count of your score. But with no one to compete against, it would just be a more sophisticated form of plinking.

FINDING YOUR LOCAL CLUB

Now that field target shooting has become so popular, there are clubs all over the country which organise regular shoots. There is a good chance that there is one within easy distance of where you live, so all you have to do is find it.

This can be harder than it sounds, however. Field target clubs don't advertise themselves in the local paper, and you won't find them in the Yellow Pages. So where do you look? The best starting point is the British Field Target Association. You will find their details in Appendix I at the back of this book. You could also have a look through the various airgun magazines. These carry regular reports on the field target scene, so you may well find a write-up on an event held by a club near you. The magazines also publish lists of clubs from time to time – such as the one in the *Airgunner Annual*, for instance.

Failing that, you could go along to your local gunsmith's shop – whose details will be in the Yellow Pages – and ask the staff there about airgun field target clubs in the area. They will probably be able to point you in the right direction, although some gunsmiths specialise in other forms of shooting such as clay pigeon shooting with shotguns, or target shooting with cartridge rifles and pistols. There are still some gunsmiths about who think of airguns as little more than toys, and consider it beneath them to get involved in the field target scene.

Once you have the name and address or telephone number of

your local club's secretary, it's a simple matter to get in touch and ask where and when they shoot. Then all you need to do is turn up on the day.

AT THE SHOOT

Don't worry if you haven't got all the gear. There's no need to feel ashamed about being a newcomer to the sport. As with most minority sports, the people who take part are delighted to have others join their ranks, and you should have no trouble finding someone who will explain what it's all about. Do try to pick your moment carefully, however. Even the friendliest shooter will be less than helpful if you tackle him just as he goes to shoot his last target, and the organisers will be busy making sure that everything is running smoothly.

Wait for a quiet moment and then explain to one of the club officials that you haven't been to a field target shoot before, but think that you might like to take up the sport. He (or she, because field target shooting is becoming increasingly popular with ladies, too) should be able to point out someone who can show you around. You probably won't want to enter the competition at this early stage in your career, for fear of looking silly, but you may get the chance to have a few shots at a field target after the main competition is over.

WHAT SHOULD YOU BUY?

One of the mistakes that newcomers to field target shooting often make is that they go out and buy all the gear far too soon. This can be very expensive, and if you later discover that field targets aren't your cup of tea, then you have wasted a lot of hard-earned cash for no reason.

Watching a field target shoot, you might get the impression that it was a condition of entry to be dressed in full camouflage gear from head to toe, and have a rifle which has had more spent on it in tuning and customising than it cost in the first place. That is not the case, of course. You can enter a field target shoot dressed in normal, everyday clothes, with a standard, inexpensive rifle. You don't even have to use telescopic sights if you don't want to – although you'll find it difficult to make a good score without them.

Sooner or later, if you get hooked on the sport, you will want to buy a special field target rifle with all the knobs on, but for the time being you simply want to find out if it's the right sport for you. If you already own a hunting rifle, then that will do fine. If not, for the first few shoots it's best to ask a friend if you can borrow his gun. Even better, go round the course together using the same gun. Then he can talk you through the various targets, and you can learn from his experience.

Borrowing a friend's gun has another advantage. It gives you a chance to try out that make and model under real conditions, which can help you later in making up your mind which gun is most suitable for you. If possible, you should try several different guns at a real field target shoot before investing a lot of money in one particular weapon.

Entering a real competition is the only way that you will get the feeling and excitement of field target shooting, but remember that you can gain plenty of experience in the other events that are run alongside the main competition at most club meetings. There will usually be two or three side events: a long-range competition, for example, or a bird shoot, and there is nearly always a plinking range, too. These give you the opportunity to fire many more shots than you could in the main competition alone, and all the while you are adding to your experience of shooting alongside others in the atmosphere of a field target event – which is a very different matter from plinking in your back garden or hunting on your own.

Once you have decided that you want to take up field target shooting, the next step is to join your local club as a fully paid-up member. In my opinion, you should also join the BASC. You might think that the BASC isn't relevant unless you shoot live quarry, but you would be wrong. The BASC fights for the rights of *all* shooters to pursue their sport without unnecessary restrictions. With growing opposition to gun ownership in this country, organisations like the BASC need the support of all of us to ensure that we continue to enjoy the freedom to own and use airguns.

27. Competition guns and gear

I mentioned in the previous chapter that you don't need to have all the top gear in order to compete in a field target shoot. You can if you wish shoot with an inexpensive gun, wearing ordinary, everyday clothes.

Indeed, there are always a few people who seem to be 'naturals' at any sport, and can carry home the prizes using equipment that most competitors wouldn't be seen dead with. One or two of the top clay pigeon shooters, for example, prefer to shoot with battered old side-by-side shotguns instead of the gleaming purpose-built over-and-unders favoured by their competitors. And there are some excellent field target shots who use standard, inexpensive airguns which would be the laughing stock of everyone else if it wasn't for the fact that they keep winning!

The fact remains that most field target shooters spend a considerable amount of money on their guns and equipment, and for very good reasons. In any competitive sport, your equipment needs to let you get on with the job of giving your very best performance, without getting in the way or distracting you from what you are doing.

CLOTHING

Field target competitions take place outside, whatever the weather, so it stands to reason that you need warm, weather-proof clothing which will not restrict your movements. It so happens that most field target shooters are also keen on hunting when they get the chance, so they use their camouflaged hunting gear which they have already, and which does the job as well as anything. After all, there is little point in going out and buying a second set of outdoor shooting clothes specially for field target shooting when you already own some.

It is worth taking some trouble over the clothes you wear for field target shooting. The requirements for field target clothing are virtually identical to those for hunting clothes, except that there is no need to be camouflaged. You still want to keep warm and dry in any weather, but have freedom of movement so you can aim and shoot comfortably. If anything, this is even more important for field target shooting, because if you miss a rabbit or a pigeon, there will always be another chance another day. In a competition, every shot counts, and if you miss a target because you are frozen to the bone, it could lose you a valuable prize and a championship title.

Remember that several thin layers are warmer than one or two thick ones, and will also allow more flexibility because you can remove or add one thin layer at a time to 'fine tune' your clothing to suit the conditions.

You will not be moving around very much at a field target shoot, because the stands are usually close together, and you will spend most of the time either standing and watching or actually shooting. You cannot rely on physical activity to keep you warm, then, so you should dress as if you were going hide shooting.

While you are shooting, you will need to kneel or sit on the ground much of the time, and if the ground is at all wet your clothes will quickly become soaked through. It makes sense to wear totally waterproof trousers, such as the waxed cotton Barbour or Beaver trousers, to keep out the damp, otherwise you will spend the rest of the day feeling soggy from the waist down.

As an alternative, some shooters carry a waterproof mat, such as the rubber mats sold as floor mats for cars. You can then lay the mat on the ground before you sit or kneel down, to keep the wet at bay. Some people even attach the mat to their belt, so it automatically falls into position when they sit down. You may feel a bit silly with a rubber mat dangling from your belt, but not half so silly as you will feel when the seat of your trousers is soaked half-way through the day.

PELLETS AND PELLET HOLDERS

Your pellets are vitally important for field target shooting – even more so than for hunting, if that is possible. A slightly mis-shapen pellet can make the difference between winning and losing, and you can't afford to take the risk that your pellets might let you down at the vital moment.

You need to buy match quality pellets, and make sure that you do everything in your power to keep them in tip-top condition right up to the moment they leave the muzzle.

The choice of pellet shape and brand is up to you, but the important thing is to use pellets that are consistent from one to the next: not just within a single tin, but from one tin, and one batch, to another. By and large, this means buying the most expensive pellets available. If you are using .177, which most field target shooters do, you can choose from the various match pellets made specifically for competitive target shooting. In .22, the choice is more limited, because most .22 pellets are designed for plinking or hunting, but even in this calibre there are some excellent pellets available.

Having chosen a good quality pellet, you can go a step further by selecting and preparing them to give even more consistent results. Tip the tin out on a clean surface, and check every single pellet for any faults or damage. Any that aren't up to scratch can be thrown away, or kept separate for plinking or practice sessions.

You will often find odd bits of lead in among the pellets, and these should be removed so they cannot become lodged in a pellet's tail and upset its balance. Some people even go so far as to wash their pellets, and weigh every single one to make sure they are identical. You may also like to use a pellet sizer to bring all the pellets down to the same diameter.

This may sound like a lot of trouble to go to, but just one bad pellet could cause a miss at a vital stage in a competition. If you can't be bothered to go to these lengths, but want totally consistent pellets, you can buy specially prepared pellets in the form of Gunpell Clones – but be prepared to pay several times the normal price.

When you've gone to the trouble or expense (or both) of obtaining top quality pellets, you obviously need to keep them that way during the competition. Tipping them into your pocket is guaranteed to get them covered with bits of fluff and grit, as well as denting the vulnerable skirts, and even keeping them in a tin can cause damage.

The best method is to use a specially designed pellet holder. This may be attached to your gun or strapped to your arm, but to my mind this still leaves the pellets open to damage from inadvertent knocks. I prefer a rigid container such as a tobacco tin, with a soft cushioned filling which has holes cut in it at intervals. This keeps the pellets separate so they cannot knock into one another, and stops them rolling about. It also means that you cannot squash them if you should accidentally sit on the container, or bump it against something. It doesn't matter that you cannot get at the pellets quickly, because you have plenty of time to load and shoot.

THE RIFLE

At a recent field target shoot, I carried out an informal survey of the guns being used. I was amazed to find that nine out of every ten guns in evidence were Weihrauch HW77s, and a similar proportion had been customised in some way. The sport has certainly come a long way since the early days when you could see everything from a BSA Meteor to a Daystate pneumatic competing alongside one another.

People are naturally inclined to follow a fashion, and the current fashion in field target guns is to use a customised HW77. What happens is that a few of the top shooters choose a particular weapon, and the others see them winning a few competitions with it. Working on the principle 'If it's good enough for him, then it's good enough for me', they go out and buy the identical make and model, believing that it will help them to shoot more like their idols.

The Weihrauch HW77, tuned and customised by Venom Arms – a popular choice with field target shooters.

Certainly you need a gun which is powerful and accurate enough to do the job, but that still leaves you with a choice between a dozen or more really good guns.

A large part of any competitive sport is having confidence in your equipment, because without that confidence you will never achieve the state of mind which allows you to perform to the peak of your ability. This is perhaps the only valid reason for following the pack, and buying the same gun everyone else is using. But before you go out and buy the same gun as all the others, whether that happens to be an HW77 or an XR3 Turbo with go-faster stripes, stop for a minute to consider whether that is really the right gun for *you*.

One man's meat is another man's poison, as the saying goes, and a gun which suits one person down to the ground may be too heavy, too small, or balanced wrongly, for you. The best thing to do is to try out as many different guns as you can, preferably at a real field target shoot, to discover which one suits you best. This is one of the advantages of belonging to a club, because you can try other members' guns before you select your own.

The first decision to be made is what type of gun to buy – a break-barrel or underlever spring airgun, or a pneumatic. If it's a pneumatic, do you want the pump-up type or one that you charge from a cylinder? Most shooters nowadays go for the spring-powered type, and these certainly have a lot going for them. They are solid and reliable, and offer plenty of possibilities for tuning. Fixed-barrel underlever types are popular at the moment, although modern break-barrel designs are capable of being just as accurate.

Pump-up pneumatics enjoyed a brief spell of popularity, but have all but disappeared from the scene now – largely because all that frantic pumping is not conducive to accurate shooting. During a field target competition, you might have to pump three hundred strokes or so in all into a typical pump-up gun, and that is bound to raise the pulse rate of even the fittest shooter at a time when you want to be as relaxed as possible.

Pre-charged pneumatics are a different matter, however. They involve no physical effort beyond working the bolt to load a pellet, and their lack of recoil makes them an attractive proposition. Top-quality pre-charged pneumatics such as the Daystate and the Sportsmatch GC2 are set to make a big impact on the field target scene, in my opinion, so if you want to be ahead of your time perhaps that is the type to go for.

One thing that most field target shooters agree on is the calibre of their guns. Nearly everyone uses .177, for the simple reason that the flatter trajectory makes it easier to estimate the correct amount of holdover or holdunder for a give range. The potential for error is smaller than with the more curved trajectory of the heavier .22 pellet, while a .177 has more than enough power to knock a field target down, even at extreme range.

Few people can afford to have one gun for hunting and another for field target shooting, so usually the same gun will have to do both jobs. Indeed, this is a good idea, since you will become more familiar with the gun's trajectory and general performance the more you use it. Using different guns with different characteristics will only lead to confusion. This is not really a problem, since the requirements are much the same for both types of shooting. Remember that shiny plates and engraving will make it harder to conceal the gun in the field, however.

Specially built field target weapons are usually heavier than hunting rifles, since the greater weight leads to improved accuracy. Hunting guns must be a compromise, since you need to carry them in the field and too much weight would be a burden.

Another area where there can be conflict between the needs of hunting and field target shooting is fitting a silencer. Quite naturally, many people like to use a silencer in the field, since it helps them to avoid alarming their quarry. Most silencers have some effect on the gun's performance, though, however small – regardless of the claims made in the advertisements. Given a choice, I would not fit a silencer for field target shooting. It is a potential source of trouble, and adds nothing to your performance at a competition.

TUNING AND CUSTOMISING

In the pursuit of peak performance, many shooters also have their guns tuned by experts such as Airmasters or Venom. As we saw earlier in this book, this evens out the variability from one shot to the next that you inevitably get with a mass-produced weapon straight out of the box. The main aim of tuning is to make the weapon as consistent as possible, so that every shot leaves the barrel at the same velocity. Tuning can also increase the power of a gun, but beware of going over the legal 12 ft lbs limit. Quite apart from being illegal, this will also lead to you being instantly disqualified if the shoot you are entering happens to have a compulsory chronograph test. Few do at the moment, but the way things are going chronograph testing will become the rule rather than the exception over the next few years.

As well as tuning the insides of your gun, you may also want to customise the outside. Engraving, precious metal plates and so on are fine, but they do nothing to improve its performance. If you have the money and want to spend it that way, go ahead – just don't expect to shoot any better because of it.

More worthwhile to my mind is customising the stock. This may take the form of adding spacers or contoured blocks, or scrapping the original stock altogether and making a new one from scratch. In either case, the idea is to make the stock fit your body as closely and comfortably as possible, so you can shoot more accurately.

The grip of the stock, where your trigger hand goes, is one of the most important points of contact, so it figures that this part should fit your hand well. You can shape an oversized grip by cutting and filing, or if it is undersized build it up with some kind of plastic material which sets hard, such as fibreglass or plastic wood. This latter method allows you to create an absolutely perfect fit, because you can use your own hand as the mould, squeezing the material as it sets with your normal shooting grip.

Another part of the stock that can usefully be modified is the comb, or the piece where your cheekbone rests against the woodwork. Most rifles are designed so that they can be used with open sights, which demands a lower head position to align your eye with the sights. When you fit a scope, you need to raise your head to look through it properly. This means that you move your head away from the stock, and lose an important point of contact, as well as leading to the possibility of errors in bringing your head up to the same position each time.

The answer is to fit a cheekpiece or comb raiser, which can be made of any wood or plastic material shaped to fit and fixed firmly to the wood of the stock. You can experiment with raisers of different shapes and sizes until you arrive at the one which suits your shooting position and physical characteristics. Alternatively, if you are making a brand new stock from a walnut 'blank', you can make it with a raised comb and cheekpiece designed specially for shooting with a scope. One of my favourites is the Tyrolean style stock, which has a smooth hollow into which you fit your cheek. This is extremely comfortable, and ensures that your head is in the same position relative to the sights every time you bring the gun to your shoulder.

Finally, I believe that a sling is a worthwhile addition to any air rifle, particularly for the demanding conditions of a field target competition. A sling helps to steady the gun whatever position you are shooting from: prone, sitting, kneeling or standing. By locking the gun more tightly against your body, it helps to ensure that you stay on aim throughout the firing process, and minimises the effect of the vibration caused by the gun's mechanism.

Going back over all the points I have made about field target guns, it is possible to arrive at a specification for my 'ideal' weapon for the sport. It would be a pre-charged pneumatic in .177 calibre, pushing out a pellet at just a whisker under 12 ft lbs with extreme consistency. It would weight about 9 lbs, and would be perfectly balanced. It would be fitted with a good, solidly mounted telescopic sight and a sling, and it would have contoured grips and stock designed to fit me perfectly. And if I was ever lucky enough to own such a rifle, I still wouldn't become a champion because it's the man behind the rifle, not the rifle itself, that makes the difference. That's a point that you should never forget when selecting your airgun gear.

28. The competition

Let's suppose that you have followed the advice in the last three chapters, and you are now arriving at a field target shoot to compete for the first time. How does it all work? What do you have to do?

The first thing to do is enter your name as a competitor. Do this as soon as you arrive, otherwise you may find that the shoot is full before you even hand in your name. Find the official who is taking the entries, and give him your name. At a big event, the organisers will be stationed in a clubhouse or marquee, but at small club shoots you are likely to find them working from the back of an estate car, with a small sheet of paper fluttering in the breeze, on which if it kept still for long enough you would read 'entries here' or something similar.

Once the official has taken your name, you will receive a score card. This may be a smart printed form, or a simple scrap of paper with your name scribbled on it. Guard this with your life, because this is the card on which your score will be recorded, and without it you might as well never have shot at all. Next, look for a set of rules pinned up on a tentpole or noticeboard, and read them through. You may think you know them already, but something may have been changed since last time, and you don't want to be disqualified for breaking a rule you didn't know existed.

Find out whether you will be allocated a set time for shooting, or if you can shoot when you like. Squadding – the system of giving shooters fixed times when they can compete – is not common at the moment, but as the sport becomes more popular and the number of entries continues to rise, it is likely to become the norm. At this stage, you should check whether you have to shoot the targets in numerical order, or whether you can take them in the order you choose.

At some shoots you will also have to pass 'gun control', which will consist of a quick visual check of your gun to see that it conforms to the rules, and a chronograph test to measure its power. If it's over the legal limit, your day's shooting will end there and then, unless you can find someone willing to lend you his gun to compete with. Once again, this is the exception rather than the rule these days, but it is likely to become much more common in the next few years.

Competitor's rifles being checked with a chronograph before they can enter a field target competition.

CHECKING OUT THE COURSE

Your next move is to wander round the course and take a good look at all the targets. Make a mental note of how difficult each one is, and whether you can shoot it in your favourite position. Most shoots will have some targets which must be shot from the standing position, either because there is a sign to that effect, or because the target itself has been positioned in a dip so you can only see the kill zone if you stand. You can then plan how to approach the course. If you are allowed to shoot the targets in any order, you may prefer to take the hardest ones first, or perhaps shoot one or two easy ones first to boost your confidence.

Consider the weather, too. If the wind is strong, it could be worth waiting to see if it drops later in the day, for instance. Or perhaps rain is forecast, and you would do better to shoot early before it sets in.

LAST-MINUTE PRACTICE

If you have time, it's a good idea to spend a while on the plinking range, and even to enter one or two of the minor events, before you shoot the main competition. This gives you the chance to check that your gun is still zeroed in after the journey, and the sights haven't been knocked out of alignment. It's also an opportunity to have a few minutes' practice and get your eye in before tackling the main shoot. Treat your practice as seriously as you would the real thing, and use it as an opportunity to remind yourself of the basic points which are so easily forgotten in the heat of a competition – such as squeezing the trigger gently, and bringing the gun to your shoulder in the same way every time. If you will have to shoot from different positions in the main competition, make a point of practising each of them, especially the ones you are less confident about.

Once you feel good and ready, and not before, go along to the first shooting position and take your place in the queue.

AT THE FIRING POINT

At each shooting position, you will probably have to wait some time before you can shoot. Spend this time usefully by watching the shooters ahead of you, to see if you can pick up any tips, or spot any mistakes to avoid. When your turn comes, you will have to hand your score card to the scorer, so he can mark on it whether you kill or miss the target. Make sure you have everything ready before you step up to the firing position, especially if there is a time limit on the stand. Then take your time and try not to feel hurried, no matter how many other shooters are waiting behind you for their turn. If you hold on-aim too long and start to wobble, bring the gun down and rest a moment before starting again. You must treat every target as though it means the difference between winning and losing, as indeed it might turn out to later on. If you miss one target and lose the match by one point, then the most important target was the one you missed.

Remember to obey the instructions of the marshals and scorers to the letter. If someone blows the whistle to signal 'cease firing', open your gun and wait for the all clear. Don't be tempted to fire off a shot anyway because you are on-aim. You will quite rightly be disqualified, because when it comes to gun safety the organisers can't afford to allow second chances.

Very often you will have to shoot two or three targets from each firing position. Make sure the scorer knows which one you are aiming at, and check beforehand if you aren't sure whether you have to take them in numerical order. And once you have fired at each target, double check that your gun is unloaded, and open the breech, before standing up and turning round.

In most shoots you will score one point for a kill, and zero for a miss. The scorer will mark a '1' or a 'K' for a kill, and '0' or 'L' for a miss. Check your score card immediately the scorer hands it back to you. Scorers are human, and although they don't like to admit it, they can make mistakes. If you bring it to their attention at the time, any mistake can be corrected, and you have the advantage of witnesses in the shape of the other shooters queuing up behind you, who will remember whether or not you killed a particular target. If you leave it until after you have left the stand, there is no chance to have the mistake put right.

When you have completed the course, take your card back to the scoring tent and hand it in, making quite sure that it goes into the pile along with all the others. It doesn't often happen, but occasionally a card can slip down between two tables and get lost. And without a card, you might as well not have competed.

A well-run shoot will have a 'leader board' displaying the names and scores of the leading shooters so far. This adds to the excitement, because you can watch the top shots vying for first place through the day.

Even if you have no chance of winning, try to wait until the end of the day to watch the prizegiving ceremony. A prizegiving is a very flat affair if everyone but the winners has gone home, and with luck one day you will be among them. Then you will be glad if the others have waited to congratulate you on your achievement. There is much more to a field target shoot than just the shooting, and if you walk off in disgust after a poor performance, you will never gain the full enjoyment from the day. Watch the other competitors shooting, and try to pick up tips from how they approach the course. Wander round and chat to the other shooters: commiserate with one another, swap hints, compare weapons, and discuss the experiences of the day. Savour the atmosphere of the event because this is a large part of what field target shooting is all about. Winning is important, sure, but there's much to be gained from a day at a field target shoot even if you do walk home empty-handed. At least you can console yourself with the fact that a couple of hundred others won nothing, too!

29. Shooting to win

No matter how much they enjoy the atmosphere of a field target shoot, most people would admit that they would like to win. After all, that's really what any competitive sport is all about. But of the dozens or even hundreds of people who enter any field target shoot, there can only be one winner. What is it that separates the winners from the losers, and how can you improve your chances of winning?

Your equipment is important, of course, and a good rifle and pellets will certainly help. But equipment alone isn't enough. There are plenty of shooters who have superb equipment, but never make it into the top ten.

There are three main factors that separate the winners from the also-rans: skill, practice and mental attitude. Let's look at each in turn.

SKILL

A successful field target shooter must combine several different skills. He – or she – must be able to estimate range accurately, and convert that correctly into the right amount of holdover or holdunder for a given target. The shooter must then have the necessary skill in aiming and shooting the rifle to hit the targets consistently.

These skills can be learned, but there are always some people who seem to have a natural ability, and take to airgun shooting like ducks to water. These are the lucky few who don't have to work too hard at acquiring the knack. For most of us, it is necessary to develop these skills over a period of time. You can't expect to take up field target shooting one week, and be winning prizes the next.

Estimating range is something that few people can do straight away, but it is vital if you are going to succeed. You must be able to judge at a glance the distance of a field target at anything from 5 to 50 yards, and you need to be accurate to within about 5 yards to be sure of using the right holdover. Fortunately, field targets are all about the same size, so with practice it is possible to become quite accurate at judging their range. Practice is the only way to reach the level of accuracy that you need. You can practise estimating range anywhere and at any time, simply by looking at a fixed point, judging how far away it is, and then pacing out the true distance. But to develop the skill for field target shooting, the best method is to use real field targets, setting them out at different distances and practising your range estimation on the real thing.

You must remember that the human eye can easily be deceived. The brain has to interpret the messages it receives from the eyes, and to do so it makes certain assumptions based on its experience. If you look at a photograph of a building, for example, your brain assumes that it is roughly the same size as other buildings you have seen in real life. If there is a person in the photograph, towering over the building, then your brain works out that it must be a model. In the same way, the surroundings of a field target can confuse your brain into thinking that it is closer or further away than it really is. A target set out in a bare field will often look further than it really is, while one surrounded by trees and bushes may appear closer. For this reason, you should practise judging range in different situations, so you can cope with whatever the shoot organisers throw at you.

Once you have estimated the range of your target, you must then calculate the correct amount of holdover or holdunder required at that range to allow for the trajectory of your pellet.

A field target shooter checks his pellet before loading it into the breech – while the scorer checks his pen!

This sounds complicated, but it is actually quite simple once you have mapped out the trajectory of your gun as I described in Chapter 11. When you know the range, you can simply read off the correct holdover or holdunder from your graph, and if you do this often enough you will soon come to know your gun's trajectory by heart so you will not even need to refer to the graph.

**SHOOTING
POSITIONS**

Far more difficult is the business of aiming and shooting your gun. The first step is to adopt a good shooting position. The classic rifle shooting style is to lie prone – that is, flat on your stomach, with your feet slightly apart and your body at a slight angle to the line of fire. This position places the maximum area of your body in contact with the ground, giving you great stability. You place both elbows on the ground, so the rifle is supported by a rigid triangle of bone, and by using a sling you can 'lock up' this position even more firmly. Your grip on the rifle should be firm, but not so tight that your knuckles are white, otherwise your muscles will begin to shake after a short time.

Most field target shooters prefer to shoot from a sitting position, however, even though this is less stable. Part of the reason for this is that field target shoots are normally held in grass fields where shooting prone would involve firing through the long grass – unlike the well-kept ranges at Bisley, for example. The sitting position can be made stable enough, provided you adopt it properly. The point to remember is that the gun should always be supported right the way from the ground by bone in as straight a line as possible. This will allow you to hold the gun steadier than if you are supporting it by tightening your muscles. Because of the way muscles work, it is simply not possible for them to maintain a steady contraction for any length of time. After a short while, they begin to shudder, imperceptibly at first, but more noticeably as time goes by.

Remember also that the most stable shape is a tripod – with three firm points of contact with the ground. The sitting position provides this if you make full use of both legs. Sit down facing at about 45 degrees to the target. Then draw your right knee up almost to your chest. This knee provides a support for your trigger hand and the rifle's pistol grip. Your left foot should be further out in front of you, so that your left knee comes up to steady your left forearm which is supporting the rifle at the fore-end, forming another 'leg' of the tripod. If you have a sling around this arm, so much the better. Then pull the rifle firmly, but not tightly, into your shoulder, and align your head properly with the sight.

There will be some targets that must be shot from the standing position, and this is more difficult because it is less stable. Instead of the three-legged tripod effect of the sitting position, you only have two points of contact with the ground. In a strong wind, for example, you cannot help swaying – and even in a flat calm you will wobble slightly. As before, you should try to support the gun with bone rather than muscular effort. The classic standing target shooting stance is to bed your left elbow firmly into your hip, supporting the fore-end on your palm or the tips of your fingers. This means you must tilt your body at the waist in order to line up with the target. It will probably feel unnatural at first, but experience has shown that it is the most stable way to shoot standing, and it is worth

A field target shooter in the standing position – supporting his elbow on his hip to steady his aim.

persevering to get it right. Once you have got the knack, you will be able to maintain this position for several minutes at a time without tiring, because there is very little muscular effort involved.

AIMING AND FIRING

Once you are comfortably in position, line up the cross-hairs with the aiming point on the target, remembering to allow the necessary amount of holdover or holdunder. Controlling your breathing is an important part of aiming. You will find that breathing in and out causes the rifle to raise and lower. Arrange yourself so that the sights are spot on when you breathe out. Take a normal breath, slowly let it out so that the sights come onto the target, and gently squeeze the trigger.

It is natural for your body to tense as you squeeze the trigger, but you should train yourself to stay relaxed, so that it is only the trigger finger muscles that move. Some people find it helps to think in terms of squeezing the trigger and pistol grip between your finger and thumb, while others slide their trigger finger back along the inside of the trigger guard. Whatever you do, don't pull the trigger suddenly. If you feel the rifle beginning to sway off-target, bring the gun away from your shoulder and start again. If you rush to fire before the gun sways off-target, you will jerk the trigger and miss.

Following through is important. This means holding the gun on aim after you have fired. It is tempting to drop the gun away from your shoulder and look over the top of the sights immediately you have fired, to see if the target is hit. This will spoil your accuracy, however, because it will cause you to tense up immediately before you fire, and then relax as soon as the gun goes off. You will tend to start to relax before the pellet has left the muzzle, throwing the pellet off-course. Instead, try to hold your aim until the pellet strikes, watching through the scope until you see the target fall.

PRACTICE

Having the necessary skills is vital to good shooting, but as all top athletes know that is only part of the story. You must practise to develop your skills and then keep yourself at the peak of your performance, otherwise you will become rusty. Regular practice will ensure that your body learns the correct shooting positions and trigger techniques, for instance, so that you will naturally repeat them in the correct way without having to think about it.

It is easy to get into bad habits during practice sessions,

however, and once learned they can be difficult to get out of. For this reason it is vital that you take your practice seriously, and treat every shot as though it was the vital one in a competition. Do not allow yourself to develop sloppy habits in practice, because this is worse than no practice at all.

Your practice sessions should be as close as possible to the real thing. Ideally, you should buy yourself a field target or two which are identical to the type used in real competitions. Set these up at different ranges each time so you have to exercise your range judging skills as well as your marksmanship. And remember to practise all the different shooting positions, not just the one you find easiest.

Most of the top shooters practise regularly – at least once a week. A practice session can last a few minutes or several hours, but you should always be prepared to give up when you have had enough. I reckon that an hour or so is about right. After that, it is easy to lose interest and slip into a lazy way of shooting, because there isn't the pressure that you get in a real competition.

It makes sense to practise hard in the lead-up to a big competition, but don't over-do it. The day before the competition, spend half an hour or so polishing up your technique, then give yourself a rest. Practising too hard just before a competition can do more harm than good. You want to be fresh when you step up to compete, and that isn't possible if you spent eight hours the day before shooting at practice targets.

MENTAL ATTITUDE

Besides natural ability, skill and dedication, there is another factor that distinguishes the shooters who are regularly among the winners – their mental attitude. Determination to win is part of it, but there's more. The psychological factor is recognised by top sportsmen in many fields as being vital to winning in competition. It's a case of mind over matter. You must not only want to win, you must believe that you can – even will – win before you can perform at your best. An important part of this is confidence in your equipment and your own ability.

Some of the top clay pigeon shooters, for example, go through a complicated process of 'psyching' themselves up for a big competition. This is partly a matter of building confidence, and partly relaxing themselves so that they are not too tense when they come to compete. The same sort of methods are used by Olympic athletes, some of whom even employ psychologists to help them develop the right mental approach to competition.

That is probably going a bit far for field target shooting, but it is certainly true that your attitude of mind will make a big difference to your shooting. If you go along to a shoot assuming that you don't stand a chance, your attitude will be: why bother trying too hard, when I'm not going to win anyway? Subconsciously, you may even deliberately not try your hardest, so you have an excuse when you don't score very well.

Try to develop a positive mental attitude to competitions. Tell yourself that your equipment is working well, you have the ability to make a good score, and you are going to do your very best. But don't let it get you down too much if you don't win. It's a great thrill to be in among the winners, but field target shooting is about having fun. If you care too much about winning, you will often be disappointed, and you won't enjoy the sport any more. When that happens, it's time to take a long, hard look at your sport and ask yourself why you do it. Because if the fun has gone out of it, there is little point in carrying on.

30. Running a field target shoot

As an amateur sport, field target shooting is organised by people who have to earn a living elsewhere during the week, and spend much of their spare time running clubs and events. These dedicated individuals are the backbone of the sport, and without them it would grind to a halt. As your interest in field target shooting grows, you may find yourself suddenly thrown into the position where you need to help run a club, or organise a shoot. You may even decide to set up a club from scratch, if there isn't one already in your area. This can be a daunting prospect, because it places a great deal of responsibility on your shoulders. The unpaid officials who run field target clubs receive very little thanks for their efforts, but if things go wrong, there is no shortage of people to criticise them.

STARTING A CLUB

Let's suppose that your nearest club is a long way away, and you decide to set up a local club with some of your friends. How do you start? A small club can be run on a very informal basis, just a group of friends who give themselves a name, meet in the home of one of their number, or a local pub, and have a field somewhere where they can set up a few targets and run friendly competitions. But sooner or later you will want to expand, taking on new members and forming a team to compete against other clubs in the area.

That is the point where you need to get yourselves organised on a more formal basis. You need to write a set of rules for the club, and appoint officials. The British Association for Shooting and Conservation or the British Field Target Association will be able to help you with suggestions for the wording of the rules. These will start with the name of the club: 'The club shall be called The Little and District Sporting Air Rifle Club', for instance. Then there will be the aims and objectives of the club: things such as 'To promote the sport of airgun field target shooting'; 'To promote and foster a spirit of friendly competition among members'; and 'To organise field target competitions for members and their guests'.

Then come the rules about the officers of the club, which specify the official posts on the committee, and how people are to be appointed – usually by a vote at an annual general meeting. The committee will normally consist of five or six people, including a chairman who presides over the meetings, a secretary who does all the donkey work of keeping membership records and minutes of the meetings, and a treasurer who looks after the money. There may also be a committee member who is responsible for organising the shoots, and another in charge of safety. It is helpful to have all these clearly defined in the rules, because then everyone knows what their responsibilities are.

Next will be the rules of membership, which define who may become a member, and how they go about joining. Most club rules will have a clause saying that newcomers must be considered for membership by the committee, and approved at a committee meeting before they become a full member. There will also be a rule which says that members may be expelled from the club by the committee if their behaviour is considered likely to bring the sport into disrepute, or some similar wording. This allows you to kick out anyone who behaves badly at a shoot, for example.

It may begin to sound as though running a club is all to do with rules and committees, but it isn't like that at all. It is actually great fun and very rewarding, but you must have the club set up properly if it is going to thrive, and that means keeping the paperwork in order.

You should also set up a bank account for the club, so that club funds are kept separate from your own personal money. Money is always a touchy subject, so you need to keep accurate accounts which show exactly how much money has been received in subscriptions and shoot entry fees, and what it has been spent on. This can be time-consuming, which is why you need to have an official treasurer to look after the financial side of things. You will need to set a realistic membership sub-scription, because you can't run a club on thin air, and you will need to buy targets and perhaps a chronograph, and there will be postage costs in keeping your members informed about decisions taken at the committee meetings, details of forth-coming events, and so on.

Attracting new members for your club can be hard work, although it is amazing how the word seems to get around. One of the best methods is to write to the airgun magazines, explaining that you are setting up a club in the area, and giving a name and address for people to write to if they are interested in joining. The magazines can't guarantee to publish letters like this, but the editor will usually do his best to find the space and will help to publicise your club. The same applies after the club is set up and you are running shoots. Keep the editors informed about your shoots, both before and afterwards. They may be able to publish your fixtures so that more people know about the events and can come along, and a brief report of shoots that have been held is always welcome. This should include all the details of where and when it was held, how many people entered, and who the winners were. If you can send a black-and-white photograph as well, so much the better. You could even get in touch with your local paper and invite them to send a reporter along to one of of your shoots. This will help to publicise the better aspects of the sport, which will give a more balanced picture to the general public. All too often all they see of airgun shooting is reports of hooligans causing damage with airguns.

ORGANISING A SHOOT

A field target shoot can be a very informal affair, or it can be highly organised. Basically it depends on the number of people you expect to attend. For a small club meeting of a dozen members, you will need very little organisation. Scraps of paper will do for score cards, and the targets can be set up first thing in the morning and taken down once everyone has shot. For a 'friendly' competition, you may even allow shooters to mark each other's score cards, so you only need two or three 'officials'.

For a larger event, or one where there is serious competition involved, the event has to be more organised, however. A big championship can take weeks of planning, with dozens of different people each with their own responsibilities. The basic principles remain the same, though, whether it's a club 'friendly' or a national championship.

The first thing to do is decide on a date and venue. You should begin by checking whether there are any other events planned for that day, and be prepared to change your plans if there is a clash of dates. The British Field Target Association can advise you here – and indeed with most other aspects of organising a shoot.

Once you have decided on the time and place, you should immediately make plans to publicise these details to anyone who might want to shoot so that they can make a note in their diaries and avoid making other plans for that day. Make sure you give good directions on how to find the shoot, and on the day itself have plenty of signposts on the roads approaching the shoot.

Then the real work begins. The shoot day itself is just the tip of the iceberg. Beneath the surface are many long hours of hard work making all the preparations. There is a huge list of equipment and other bits and pieces that will be needed on the day. All these need to be begged, borrowed or bought, and arrangements made to have them taken to the right place the day before and set up. The list includes: direction signs; signs for the various stands and targets, as well as the car park, entry tent, plinking range, toilets and so on; a noticeboard for the rules, and the rules themselves; a blackboard and chalk to mark up the scores of the leading shooters throughout the day; tents or marquees; chemical toilets; refreshments; yards and yards of tape or rope and posts to mark off danger areas and the firing line; the targets for the main shoot, with plenty of cord for resetting them, with plenty of cord for resetting them, and spares in case one or two should go wrong; targets for the side events such as the plinking range; a chronograph for testing competitors' rifles; score cards and score sheets; a clipboard, pen, whistle and armband for each scorer and official; a cash tin with a 'float' of change; the prizes themselves; and plenty of tools such as pliers, string, wire, hammers and nails to fix signs and so on. The list could go on and on. You might want a public address system, or walkie-talkie radios, to help control an event spread out over a large area, for instance. There may be trade stands set up by local gunshops, or sponsors to consider. Experience will teach you what you need, and by starting with small, simple events you can build up slowly to the larger ones.

The important thing is to make sure that everyone knows what their job is. You need one person designated as the overall organiser, who co-ordinates the efforts of all the others. The organiser should have nothing to set up himself, so that he is free to be in overall charge – that is a full-time job in itself.

Long before the shoot itself, you should have a meeting of all those involved to decide who will be responsible for what. Visit the site and plan where everything will go, drawing a map to show where you plan to site the car park, tents, firing points and so on. This will help you to make sure that nothing is missed, and avoids any last-minute problems when you discover that the field isn't big enough for everything you want to do. Remember to allow for bad weather. If you are planning to park the cars on a field, for instance, consider what the alternatives are if the ground is too wet on the day.

One important point to consider is insurance. Naturally you hope that no one will be hurt, and you will do everything you can to see that safety rules are set and adhered to. But there is always a remote chance that someone could be injured – even if they simply stub their toe on a tent peg. As the organiser of an event, you could be held liable for damages so you need to arrange public liability insurance for the club. This should not prove too expensive, and can be arranged quite simply through an insurance broker. The BASC provides insurance cover for its members, and would be able to advise clubs on their insurance needs.

So far as the shooters are concerned, one of the most important aspects of the day is the targets themselves and the way they are set out. As an organiser, it is tempting to make the targets very difficult, to make sure of separating out the top shooters. You should remember, however, that most of the people who compete stand little chance of winning. They come to enjoy the day, and it won't be much fun for them if they only score two out of twenty. You should make most of the targets relatively straightforward, keeping them within reasonable range and adding interest by placing some of them among cover, or in trees. You will need one or two difficult, long-range targets, but very close targets can be just as difficult to hit, and they add to the variety. You will be surprised at how many shooters miss even the simplest targets, and only a very few will come near to making a perfect score. If you end up with two or three shooters tied for first place at the end of the day, a shoot-off for first prize adds a great deal of excitement, and gives the other shooters a chance to watch the top competitors battling it out under pressure.

Field target shooting is not a great spectator sport, but you should spare a thought for those who come to watch rather than take part. There will be wives and girlfriends, parents and people who are thinking of taking up the sport, as well as shooters who have finished the course and want to see how others are doing. Make sure that they can watch the action without getting in the way, and try to provide them with somewhere they can sit and have a cup of tea and still feel as though they are involved in the day.

As a part of this, a leader board showing the names and scores of the leading shooters throughout the day helps people to know how the shoot is progressing, and allows spectators to feel as though they are involved. It also means that shooters can see where they are positioned, or what score they have to beat, and adds to the excitement of the day.

The prizegiving ceremony should be a natural conclusion to the day's proceedings, giving everyone the chance to see the winners and congratulate them on their performance. All too often at shoots nowadays the ceremony takes place long after most people have set off for home. I feel that the time of the ceremony should posted on the noticeboard, and it should go ahead at that time come what may – even if that means that some people who turn up later in the day aren't able to compete.

Entries for field target shoots can easily get out of hand, and it is usually necessary to restrict the entry to a number that the organisers feel able to cope with comfortably in the time available. This is only fair to everyone, because trying to cram too many shooters through the system in a limited time only spoils the event. Clay pigeon shoots usually have a restricted entry of so many shooters, or a time after which no more entries are taken. This ensures that everyone gets a chance to shoot, and those who turn up late don't hold up the proceedings for everyone else.

It may also be necessary to set a time limit for the targets, to ensure that a slow shooter cannot clog up the course by taking ages at each firing point. One way to do this is to have a rule which says that a marshal may impose a time limit on any shooter at his discretion, giving him thirty seconds to take a shot otherwise he will record a 'miss'. This way shooters don't feel as though they are shooting against the clock, but a very slow shooter can be hurried along if necessary.

Action at a typical field target shoot. Note the ropes to keep spectators and shooters apart.

Another way of smoothing things along is to use a system of 'squadding'. This involves putting shooters into squads of five or six people who are then given a set time to begin shooting. The squads and their start times are posted on a noticeboard in the entries tent for all to see. This system has many advantages, to my mind. First, it avoids the lengthy queues which can form as shooters wait their turn. Secondly, it means that the shooters can go off and enjoy the other attractions of the day, knowing that they must return at a given time to compete. And thirdly, it allows spectators and other shooters to watch particular competitors, since they know where and when they will be shooting. The only drawback to squadding is that people may want to shoot earlier or later in the day because of a change in the weather – but I reckon that is just the luck of the draw, and is something that shooters will have to accept if they want their sport to thrive.

Safety is a vital part of any field target event, and there should be one official whose sole responsibility is to see that the shoot is run safely. Firing points and targets should be planned out with safety in mind from the start, and all the scorers and marshals should be thoroughly briefed on safety procedures beforehand. You should make sure that all the competitors are aware of the safety rules, perhaps by printing them on the score cards. These should include a rule to the effect that guns may only be loaded and fired from a designated firing point, in the presence of an official, and that shooters must follow the instructions of officials at all times. All firing must stop, and guns must be unloaded, when a whistle is blown – when a target needs to be mended, for instance. Anyone breaking one of these rules must be disqualified from the shoot instantly, and asked to leave the ground. You can't afford to give people second chances when it comes to safety.

I have mentioned before that I believe chronograph testing should be compulsory at all shoots, to ensure that all rifles being used are within the law. This is vital if the sport is to avoid bad publicity, and it also avoids the bitter arguments that can ensue when someone is accused of competing with an 'over the limit' gun.

SPONSORSHIP

I have left sponsorship until last because you cannot expect to obtain sponsorship until you have got a well organised, popular shoot. Sponsorship can be very valuable, especially with a sport which is young and struggling to survive on limited funds. But commercial companies don't give money away for nothing.

They need to know that they will get something in return in terms of associating their name with a prestigious event, and gaining publicity for their products.

The most obvious place to look for sponsorship is companies already involved with field airgun shooting, and those which gain their living from it. These include the gun and pellet manufacturers, local gunshops and the like. When you have a big, prestigious event, you can look beyond these to companies in other fields. Some shoots have been sponsored by local branches of building societies and banks, for example.

Approaching a company for sponsorship is not difficult, but it takes a bit of bare-faced cheek and you must do it in a business-like way. It is no good walking up to the counter and talking to an assistant; you must deal with the boss. Telephone first, to explain briefly what you are after and try to arrange an appointment to see him or her. When you go along, take a written proposal which sets out what you want, and what you can give in return. You might want a gun as a prize, for example, or a cash contribution towards the cost of running the event. In return, you can offer publicity. You can name the event after the sponsor, calling it the ABC Bank Field Target Trophy, for instance. You can display posters and banners at the shoot to publicise the name of the sponsor, and you can print their name and logo on the score cards. You can try to get reports of the shoot printed in the airgun magazines, naming the sponsor, and you can ask a journalist from the local paper to come to the event. All these things provide useful publicity for a company, and the more you can offer, the better chance you stand of getting the sponsorship you need.

Already many of the manufacturers and gunshops have been very generous in sponsoring field target events, and this has been vital in getting the sport to the position it is in today. If field target shooting is going to continue to thrive and grow, sponsorship will become increasingly important but organisers must be willing and able to provide sponsors with value for money, just as though they were selling advertising space on posters or in a magazine.

Appendices

Appendix I: Clubs and Organisations

Airgun clubs are too numerous to mention here, and their details are constantly changing. For information about clubs in your area, contact:

British Field Target Association

Chairman: Mrs Chris Everett
             44 Walford Way
             Coggeshall
             nr Colchester
             Essex CO6 1PF

             Tel: 0376 62472

Clubs affiliated to the BFTA are split into regions: Scotland, South-West, South Wales, North-East, North-West and East Anglia. A Midlands region is planned at the time of writing.

British Association for Shooting and Conservation
National Headquarters
Marford Mill
Rossett
Wrexham
Clwyd LL12 0HL

Tel: 0244 570881

The BASC is the national representative body for sporting shooting, looking after the interests of all kinds of shooters including airgunners as well as shotgun shooters.

National Smallbore Rifle Association
Lord Roberts House
Bisley Camp
Brookwood
Woking
Surrey GU24 0NP

Tel: 04867 6969

The NSRA is the governing body for smallbore and target airgun shooting in the UK. It organises the national air weapons championships for indoor target shooters, but has little to do with field target shooting.

Appendix II: Bibliography

MAGAZINES

Air Gunner (Monthly)
Romsey Publishing Company
Hill House
Heckfield
Basingstoke
Hampshire RG27 0JY

Editor: Paul Dobson
Tel: 0734 326 668

Airgun World (Monthly)
Burlington Publishing Company
10 Sheet Street
Windsor
Berkshire SL4 1BG

Editor: John Fletcher
Tel: 07535 56061

Guns Review (Monthly)
Broad Stone
Heptonstall
Hebden Bridge
West Yorkshire HX7 7PH

Editor: C. Greenwood
Tel: 0422 844387

Guns & Weapons User (Quarterly)
73–75 Goswell Road
London EC1 7SN

Editor: Marcus Dobbs
Tel: 01–250 1944

Shooting & Conservation (Quarterly)
(The magazine of the BASC,
details in Appendix I) Editor: James McKay

Appendix III: Facts and Figures

To calculate the muzzle energy of an airgun

$$\text{Energy (ft lbs)} = \frac{\text{Velocity (feet per sec)}^2 \times \text{Pellet weight (grains)}}{450,240}$$

For example, a rifle with a muzzle velocity of 600fps with .22 calibre Eley Wasp pellets weighing 14.5 grains:

$$\frac{600^2 \times 14.5}{450,240} = 11.59 \text{ ft lbs}$$

Some typical pellet weights

.177 calibre

		.22 calibre	
Silver Jet	8.2 grains	Silver Jet	15.2
BSA Pylarm	7.4	BSA Pylarm	14.5
Eley Wasp	7.4	Eley Wasp	14.5
H&N Match	7.7	H&N Match	12.8
RWS Hobby	6.9	RWS Hobby	11.9
RWS Squirrel	8.4	RWS Squirrel	14.1
Webley GP	7.2	Webley GP	14.2
		NATO Bullet	16.4

.20 calibre

.25 calibre

Silver Jet	12.1	
H&N Match	10.2	Champion	19.6

Calculating the exit pupil of a scope

The exit pupil is the size of the image thrown by a scope. You can see this by pointing the scope at the sky, and holding the ocular lens a few inches away from a piece of white paper. The maximum size of the pupil of the human eye is 7mm.

$$\text{Exit pupil (millimetres)} = \frac{\text{Object lens diameter (millimetres)}}{\text{Power of magnification}}$$

So for a 4 x 32 scope, the exit pupil is $\frac{32}{4} = 8mm$

Conversion factors: Pounds to kilograms 1lb = 0.454kg
Ounces to grams 1oz = 28.35g
Grams to grains 1 grain = 0.0648 gram
Feet per second to metres per second 1fps = 0.305 m/s
Yards to metres 1yd = .91m
Inches to centimetres 1in = 2.54cm

Index

Numbers in bold type refer to illustrations